# Makers of Psychology

## The Personal Factor

**Harvey Mindess**

**Antioch University**
**Venice, California**

**INSIGHT BOOKS**
**HUMAN SCIENCES PRESS, INC.**

## For Jane

Printed in the United States of America
987654321

**Library of Congress Cataloging-in-Publication Data**

Mindess, Harvey, 1928–
  Makers of psychology.

  Includes index.
  1. Psychology—Philosophy.   2. Psychologists—
Psychology.   I. Title.
BF38.M57   1988      150.19      87-4148
ISBN 0898853710 (cloth)
      089885380X (paper)

# Contents

*Acknowledgments*                                                7

1. INTRODUCTION: THE TRUE BELIEVER IN
   PSYCHOLOGY                                                    11
   An Overview of the Field                                      11
   Leaders, Followers, and Consumers as
   True Believers                                                13
   In Their Image: A Statement of My Thesis                      15

2. A PERSONAL NOTE                                               18
   My Qualifications and Idiosyncracies                          18
   The Objections to My Approach: Why
   They Are Wrong                                                23

3. THE FORERUNNERS: WUNDT AND JAMES                              27
   At the Outset: Psychology in Two
   Perspectives                                                  27
   The World of Wilhelm Wundt: A System of
   Building Blocks                                               30
   William James: A Flowing Stream                               35
   "The Elements" versus "The Stream:" An
   Augury of the Forks of the Future                             44

4. PERSONALITY THEORY AS AN INKBLOT     45
The Sources of Personality Theories: Their
Authors' Traits     45
Sigmund Freud and Psychoanalysis     47
C.G. Jung and Analytical Psychology     65

5. THE DENIAL OF PERSONALITY     84
The Personality That Denies Personality     85
Skinner's Background and Personal
Development     87
The Dark Year in Scranton     90
The Complete Behaviorist     94

6. PSYCHOTHERAPY AS AN ART FORM     110
Therapy Both a Science and an Art     111
Carl Rogers and Client-Centered
Counseling     112
Milton H. Erickson and Autohypnosis     132

7. A CASE IN POINT     147
The Case of Alice W. As Treated By Freud     147
By Jung     155
By a Behaviorist     159
By Rogers     161
By Erickson     164
By the Author     167

8. CONCLUSION: PSYCHOLOGY AS A HUMAN
UNDERTAKING     169
A Restatement of My Thesis: Its
Implications     169

References     175
Index     177

# Acknowledgments

The author and publisher wish to thank the following for permission to quote from their published works:

Jason Aronson Publishing Co. for permission to quote from Robert D. Stolorow and George E. Atwood, *Faces in a Cloud*, 1979.

Atheneum Publishing Co. for permission to quote from Vincent Brome, *Jung: Man and Myth*, 1981

Basic Books Publishing Co. for permission to quote from Ernest Jones, *The Life and Work of Sigmund Freud*, 1961.

Dell Publishing Co. for permission to quote from Howard Kirschenbaum, *On Becoming Carl Rogers*, 1979.

Alan C. Elms for permission to quote from ''Skinner's Dark Year and Walden Two,'' American Psychologist, May 1981.

Harper & Row Publishing Co. for permission to quote from Miller and Buckhout, Psychology: The Science of Mental Life, 1973.

Holt, Rinehart, & Winston Publishing Co. for permission to quote from Christopher Monte, *Beneath the Mask*, 1980.

Houghton Mifflin Publishing Co. for permission to quote from Carl R. Rogers, *A Way of Being*, 1980.

Irvington Publishing Co. for permission to quote from Ernest Rossi, Ed., *Collected Papers of Milton H. Erickson*, 1980, and Ernest Rossi et al., *Healing in Hypnosis*

Alfred A. Knopf Publishing Co. for permission to quote from F. O. Matthiessen, *The James Family*, 1947; B. F. Skinner, *Particulars of My Life*, 1976; B. F. Skinner, *The Shaping of a Behaviorist*, 1979; and B. F. Skinner, *A Matter of Consequences*, 1983.

Macmillan Publishing Co. for permission to quote from William James, *The Varieties of Religious Experience*, 1961; B. F. Skinner, *Science and Human Behavior*, 1953; and B. F. Skinner, *Walden Two*, 1948.

Norton Publishing Co. for permission to quote from Sidney Rosen, *My Voice Will Go with You: The Teaching Tales of Milton H. Erickson*, 1982.

Random House Publishing Co. for permission to quote from C. G. Jung, *Memories, Dreams, Reflections*, 1961.

Every secret of a writer's soul, every experience of his life, every quality of his mind is written large in his works.

—Virginia Woolf

An artist, great or small, works for the salvation of his own soul above all other things.       —J. Middleton Murry

I have gradually come to understand what every great philosophy . . . has been: the confession of its author and a kind of involuntary, unconscious memoir.       —Friedrich Nietzsche

There is no history—only biography.   —Ralph Waldo Emerson

# 1

# Introduction
## The True Believer in Psychology

### AN OVERVIEW OF THE FIELD

As a formal professional discipline, psychology is little more than 100 years old. It began at the university of Leipzig, where Wilhelm Wundt established the first psychological laboratory in 1879. Spreading to America as well as England, France, and other European countries, catapulted into notoriety by Sigmund Freud in Vienna around the turn of the century, it soon became what it is today—a thriving and challenging field, a cauldron of controversy, and the source of ideas that have changed the world.

Less than a generation ago, the popular image of a psychologist in America depicted him as a male, bearded, bespectacled, with a slightly stilted manner, soft-spoken and thoughtful but not very worldly. Because of the increasing exposure of pop psychologists in the 1980s, however, this image is now augmented by the vision of an attractive female, articulate and charming, quick to give advice and ready to deliver opinions on sex, love, relationships, and getting in touch with your true self at the drop of a cue card.

Like most public stereotypes, these portraits are not without a semblance of reality. Nevertheless, they are overdrawn. Besides, they fail to capture the diversity of the profession. Psychologists share certain educational backgrounds, spheres of interest, and professional mannerisms, but as personalities they range across the entire human spectrum. They include both stolid and flamboyant characters, brilliant intellects and plodders, persons of high integrity and irresponsible narcissists, compassionate souls and steely-eyed manipulators, aggressive, passive, and passive-aggressive individuals, neurotic and even psychotic cases. On the whole, however, they are remarkably normal, tied into the lifestyles of the parts of the nation in which they live, and no more problem-free than other segments of the population.

Despite this diversity of psychologists, however, one of their most striking characteristics is the fact that they cluster into warring camps. Researchers and clinicians, for example, have often been sharply opposed in their views on how psychologists should be trained. Researchers contend that they should be trained in the scientific method, well versed in statistics, and ready to avail themselves of computer technology. Clinicians, in contrast, maintain that the cultivation of empathy, genuineness, and insight into the unconscious are as important as scientific objectivity. Within the areas of psychotherapy and personality theory, moreover, Freudians vie with Adlerians and Jungians; existentialists cross swords with behaviorists; family systems practitioners decry the supposedly outmoded efforts of practitioners of individual psychotherapy; cognitive therapists, Gestalt therapists, and Rogerians are all at odds with each other; transpersonalists are ridiculed by those who believe they represent a reversion to magical thinking, while they in turn look down on the crass materialism and rigid rationalism of their opponents.

This fact—that psychology is anything but a unified field of endeavor, that psychologists are anything but united in their theories, beliefs, and methods, and that many defend their particular points of view with righteous fervor—is the launching pad from which this book takes off. It is my aim to show how psychology is made, how the theories and techniques that prevail are created; but in the process we will also see why the field is a battleground of hotly held positions.

## LEADERS, FOLLOWERS, AND CONSUMERS AS TRUE BELIEVERS

For purposes of discussion, we may divide the profession into its leaders, their followers, and its consumers. The fervor to which I refer is engendered in all three groups to greater or lesser extent, but I intend to focus on the leaders because they are the fountainhead from which the discipline is born and in them we see most clearly why psychology has assumed such diverse and conflicting forms.

How did these leaders arrive at their distinctive contributions? Freud, we all know, focused attention on the importance of sexual dynamics, first in neurosis, then in the conduct of our lives in general. He did not, however, pose the question academically— "How important is sex?" or, "What part does sex play in neurosis?"—and set out to find the answer. He simply began to believe, at one stage in his career, that he had discovered its significance, and spent the rest of his life enlarging upon this discovery. Similarly, Skinner did not begin by wondering idly how much of our behavior is due to conditioning. Rather, he found himself irresistibly attracted to behaviorism as an explanatory system and spent the rest of *his* life trying to carry it as far as he could.

"Irresistibly attracted" is the key. When a psychologist, leader or follower, is gripped by a point of view, impressed by a theory or technique, he or she tends to fall in love with it. To become infatuated with an explanation of human behavior or a method of helping us deal with our problems is as common within the field as romantic infatuation is in the world at large. It may also extend to consumers, who at various times in their lives may come under the spell of psychoanalysis, Jungian theory, or existentialist argument, imagining that all their deepest concerns can be laid to rest by the lullabies of their particular mentors.

The infatuation of disciples—be they professional psychologists or students, clients, or other laypersons who have been impressed with a leader's contributions—is itself a phenomenon of note. It derives from our common needs for explanation and inspiration, for getting a handle on the complexities of our lives and being roused out of our mental torpor by the thrill of enlightenment. Every prominent psychologist offers us such an opportunity. His or her system of thought and method of therapy appear to contain the answers to our questions, the solutions to our problems. Falling for them, therefore, in the sense of seeing them not as representing merely *another* point of view, but a *wonderful* point of view, perhaps the *best* point of view we have ever come across, is an understandable temptation.

Identification with an admired leader also counteracts the nagging feelings of inadequacy many of us carry throughout life. If I conceive of myself as a Freudian or Jungian, Rogerian, Skinnerian, or any other kind of "ian," I partake of my teacher's qualities. No longer am I merely my little bewildered self; I am now a member of an august group, a carrier of the torch of truth that was lit by my master to help humanity find its way through the night. It is one of the paradoxes of the human condition that, as we feel more complete when we lose ourselves in love for another person, we can feel more content with ourselves when we give up our critical judgment in adopting our teachers' ideas.

The paradox, however, may be more apparent than real. If we pursue the question of why we each tend to fall in love with a particular psychologist—why, for some of us, Jung represents the most profound of teachers while, for others, it is Skinner or Freud or someone else—we frequently discover that the ones we adore have either articulated positions that support our own value systems or have shed light on the very problems with which we have been silently struggling.

I remember when I fell in love with Jung. I was an undergraduate primarily interested in literature, and had only been exposed to psychology from a behaviorist point of view. The study of human nature was fascinating to me, but the behaviorist outlook seemed cramped. It portrayed human beings as mechanisms rather than mysteries, as manipulable creatures rather than players in the games of destiny. Jung was the first psychologist I came across whose breadth of vision seemed commensurate with Shakespeare's, Melville's, or Dostoyevski's. I went for him immediately because he struck me as a kindred soul. Similarly, most of the mentors we choose lend credibility to our personal inclinations; therefore adopting their ideas may not be so much a matter of giving up our critical judgment as one of linking ourselves to their eloquence.

Be that as it may, the question on which I propose to focus is why these psychologists themselves, these creative geniuses and leaders of the field, espouse the specific doctrines that come to be associated with their names. How and why do they formulate the systems that they spend the rest of their lives expounding? Concentration on this question will bring us to the heart of the matter. As we examine the careers of several great psychologists and consider the mixture of truth and error to which each one subscribed, we will see how they were constrained to look at life from peculiar, personally motivated points of view. While learning what these men had to teach us, we will also learn what drove them to teach us what they did.

## IN THEIR IMAGE: A STATEMENT OF MY THESIS

It is my intention to show how the leaders of the field portray humanity in their own image and how each one's theories and techniques are a means of validating his own identity. Freudian man, we will see, is very much like Freud himself; Jungian man is much like Jung, and so on down the line. In Nietzsche's words, each one of their philosophies is "the confession of its author." Furthermore, in creating their portraits of human nature as similar to themselves, every leader we discuss (and by implication, every other psychologist, too) gives himself a boost of self-clarification and self-acceptance. As Middleton Murry said of the artist, each one of us "works for the salvation of his own soul above all other things."

My analyses, however, are not intended to discredit the astuteness or integrity of these thinkers. We all perceive the world through our own eyes and interpret its significance in the light of our own experience. We all need to boost our self-confidence, too. The only target I wish to attack is the delusion that psychologists' judgments are objective, their pronouncements unbiased, their methods based more upon external evidence than personal need. Even the greatest geniuses are human beings, limited by the time and place of their existence and, above all, limited by their personal characteristics. Their outlooks are shaped by who they are. There is no shame in that, but it is a crime against truth to deny it.

This obvious fact explains why no psychologist has ever commanded the allegiance of the entire profession and why no method of psychotherapy has ever helped all who sought its benefits. The field as a whole, taking direction as it does from the standpoints of its leaders—which, as I will demonstrate, are *always* personally motivated—may be regarded as a set of distorting mirrors, each one reflecting human nature in a somewhat lopsided way, with no guarantee that all of them put together add up to a rounded portrait. It may be going too far to say that psychologists succeed in enlightening and helping us only to the extent that our preoccupations and problems coincide with theirs; but it is not going *much* too far.

The benefits we can possibly derive from psychotherapy must also be brought into question. What we obtain depends, at least in part, on whom we consult; and every therapist is limited by his or her self. To put all our faith in their guidance, therefore, is to chase a mirage. True, they can give us support, help us sort through our feelings and acquire new ways of dealing with our lives. Nevertheless, if we are to be faithful to ourselves, in the end we must find our own solutions and fashion our own deliverance. The most intelligent attitude with which to face our therapists is one of respectful skepticism. While following their guidance and opening ourselves to their suggestions, we must never forget that at base their truths are just that—*their* truths, which work, we can only hope, for *them,* but not necessarily for us.

Sometimes we may find, to our dismay, that our therapists' truths do not even work for them. Their personal lives may be in greater disarray than those of their clients. When that is the case, it seems naive to accept their guidance, though many troubled persons, albeit often unwittingly, are treading that questionable path at this very moment, as they have done throughout the history of the field.

Fortunately, however, the psychologists we will discuss created truths that did work for them. Each one, as we will see, found fulfillment in his own way. Nevertheless, that still leaves our essential concern unanswered. How far can the teachings of the leaders of the field lead *us?* How much of Freud shall we accept? How much of Jung, Rogers, Skinner, Erickson, and the rest? By examining their lives and works, we will see where they were shortsighted, where their personal needs overshadowed their judgment. These analyses will help us draw the line in our acceptance of their doctrines.

More provocatively, perhaps, these analyses should make it clear that for any intelligent person to call himself a Freudian, Jungian, Rogerian, Skinnerian, Ericksonian, or "ian" of any kind is tantamount to confessing that he has not penetrated to his own core of self-understanding and self-acceptance. One may legitimately be impressed with a leader's teachings, find him or her a brilliant preceptor and enlightener of certain areas of experience. To be a true believer in psychology or psychologists, however, to give unquestioning allegiance to any one person's outlook or to the field as a whole, is to avoid the very challenge that made its leaders great—the challenge to fashion one's own unique and inimitable identity.

Despite the strain of skepticism that clearly runs through this book, I do not wish to give the impression that it is primarily a work of criticism. It is really one of appreciation. I admire these people and marvel at their achievements, as I love the field of psychology, for all its inherent shortcomings. We do the leaders of the profession homage, I feel, by scrutinizing them as unflinchingly as they scrutinized the human race. There is something inspiring in seeing a person create a lifework and through it achieve a sense of self-validation. There is also something breathtaking in seeing how objectivity and subjectivity merge, how today's truth is tomorrow's error, how one person's pathway into light is another person's endless maze. While remaining as incredulous as I am, therefore, I hope to convey the wonder of it all, which is the wonder of our common humanity.

# 2

# A Personal Note

Let me explain how I came to be interested in this topic and why I have organized this book in the way I have.

## My Qualifications and Idiosyncrasies

I have been a psychologist for over 30 years. I received my formal education at UCLA, whose department was entrenched in behaviorist doctrine. Their standpoint did not appeal to me, so with other disgruntled students, I attached myself to a maverick professor, Bruno Klopfer, expert in the Rorschach technique and a Jungian analyst to boot. For years I made my living interpreting inkblots. That experience left a deep impression on me. I came to believe that the world is our inkblot, that to some extent we all project the forms and contents of our own minds onto every one we meet and everything we see. That notion is the root of my thesis that psychologists see humanity in their own image.

After leaving UCLA, I received a fellowship to study at the C. G. Jung Institute in Zurich. I met Jung and had a memorable conversation with him which I will recount in due time, but I became so disillusioned with his disciples that I left the Institute without completing my training. Subsequently, I was employed at Cedars-Sinai Hospital in Los Angeles, where the psychiatric bias was distinctly Freudian. Finding myself at odds with this stance too, I finally came to see that I was an inveterate skeptic, that I could never be a true believer in any school of psychology or in psychology as a whole. It seemed to me that the schools were cults oblivious to any truths except their own and the field was a mishmash of strident pronouncements, large areas of obscurity, and beliefs lacking substance beyond the convictions of their proponents.

At that point, I became involved in the study of humor. I soon felt that a humorous, or at least ironic, point of view was necessary to maintain my integrity while practicing a profession about whose ultimate significance I was doubtful. I wrote a poem expressing this outlook, which was published in *American Psychologist* (May, 1975) and brought me hundreds of letters from colleagues who shared my views. It was called, "Hail to the Chiefs," and for your amusement (I hope), here it is.

Come listen colleagues, while I relate
A story that we can celebrate;
It all began with Sigmund Freud,
A man who thoroughly annoyed
The doctors of his time and place
Because he told them to their face
That all their patients, nervous wrecks,
Were suffering from screwed-up sex.

Instead of chasing cute young yummies,
Men were dreaming of their mommies,
And women, picking up the fad,
Were making plays for dear old dad.
So though it sounds like Greek to us,
Freud said, "Zeir problem iss Oedipus!"
"I'll cure zem," he vowed, "And to sveeten ze bargain,
I'll srow in zum high-cless fency jargon."

Repression, regression, reaction formation,
Denial, avoidance, and rationalization,
Projection, undoing, and compensation,

Acting out and sublimation:
If it weren't for Freud, where would we be,
When it comes to talking about you and me?

And then along came C. G. Jung,
Whose sensibilities were stoong
To the very core by people's problems,
Because he believed they were caused by goblins
And other strange creatures whose eerie screams
Resounded through nightmarish dreams
In which ancient gods and demons battled
Until the dreamer's brains were rattled.

"To explain it," said Jung, sitting back on his haunches,
"I sink I'll invent ze collective unconscious.
I know my momma vill be overchoyed
If I can manetch to top old Freud."
No sooner said, of course, than done,
And then he added, one by one,
The thoughts that were to make us sure
That he was deep, or at least obscure.

Anima, animus, shadow, and Self,
The fairy realm of witch and elf,
Introvert, extrovert, archetype:
For terms like these the world was ripe,
And riper it grows and that's no maybe—
We've really come a long way, baby!

Meanwhile, on the ranch, our own Carl Rogers
Had devised a system by which old codgers
And young snippets too could gain relief
Without any odd European belief
In archetypes or Oedipus—
In other words, with little fuss,
Less muss, no depth, and far fewer riddles,
We all could become as fit as fiddles.

Carl called his therapy nondirective,
Then directed to his students to be reflective.
"Not in terms of thinking," he told his hearers,
"But in terms of acting like plate-glass mirrors."

Repeat, repeat what your clients say;
That's counseling in the Rogerian way.
It was later found, in a study by Garrett,
That Rogers was really a green-breasted parrot.

Nevertheless, to his great credit,
He gave us easy words to edit.
Client-centered, open, and trust,
Becoming, process, is all we must
Learn to earn (and it's not hard)
Carl Rogers's positive regard.

That brings us round to Frederick Perls,
Whose penchant for pinching the bottoms of girls
Made lechery a therapeutic style
And encouraged those shrinks who know what's worthwhile
To develop it into an art of their own,
An art that the world had never known—
For where has there ever before been a doctor
Who charged his patient while he foctor?

"I do my sing and you do yours!"
Snickered Perls, addressing the freaked-out boors
Who sat at his feet, devouring blintzes.
"Loose your mind and come to your sintzes!"
They nodded, they swayed in perfect rhythm
To let him know that they were with'm.
"Effery act iss natural, including sodomy!"
They rose in unison, chanting "Autonomy!"

Despite nasty rumors, Fritz was not too far gone
To engage in the game of inventing jar-gone.
He called his treatment style Gestalt
And won the prize (not by default)
For being the most authentic conner
In the here and now—which is quite an honor.

Finally, though, we have B. F. Skinner.
No doubt about it; he's the winner.
His cunning methods of shaping behavior
Have qualified Him as the latest Saviour.
While He explains human motivation

As well as a pigeon explains The Creation,
He has won the unqualified endorsement
Of S\*C\*I\*E\*N\*C\*E\* for naming reinforcement

The be-all and end-all of everything—
What Kant might have called Das Dingaling-
An-Sich. Besides which, He wrote Walden Two,
Which gives Him an edge over me and you.
So even if He cannot tolerate
To see a patient, we nominate
Him titular head of Behavior Mod,
The therapy that's next to God.

Desensitization and reconditioning,
Operant, classical, now He's petitioning
To be anointed in a hurry.
But never fear; we need not worry.
When Skinner is crowned King of Dreams (or REMS),
We'll all be rewarded with M&Ms.

There are others, of course, but these are our heroes,
And while some may say they're a bunch of zeroes,
I submit that their therapeutic preachments
Deserve neither censure nor impeachments.
Man (and woman) kind might not be worse off without them,
But the most magnificent thing about them
Is the fact that they labored without misgiving
So you and I could make a living.

Eventually, I was invited to create a department of psychology at Antioch University in Los Angeles, and during my 13 years there I have been teaching, among other things, the history of the field. In tracing and retracing the development of psychology from its beginnings to the present, I came to the conclusion that its leaders were without exception fallible human beings—people, that is, with their own problems, obsessions, and blind spots. No surprise, you may say, except when you see that these problems, obsessions, and blind spots are part and parcel of their contributions to the discipline. This is not, I must add, all to the bad, for a preoccupation—even a neurotic preoccupation—with a certain aspect of life and an intense need to validate a certain point of view, often lead to remarkable insights (as the literary critic

John W. Aldridge said, "You see *less,* but what you see, you see more clearly"). They may also, however, lead to remarkable dogmatism, and added all together, they show the field progressing in fits and starts, swayed this way and that by the brilliant, charismatic personalities who have dominated it at various stages of its development.

## THE OBJECTIONS TO MY APPROACH: WHY THEY ARE WRONG

My approach in this book falls under the rubric of an endeavor known as psychobiography, and there are those, I well know, who object to this entire enterprise. Examining a creative genius's output in relation to his or her personal life seems, to these critics, either beside the point or a degradation of the person's achievement. If I show that Freud, for instance, had a peculiar set of sexual needs that played an important part in his lifelong preoccupation with sexual psychodynamics, it would be said that I am dwelling on matters that do not matter, or worse, that by exposing Freud's neurotic tendencies I am demeaning his greatness.

This objection originally arose in response to some psychologists' attempts to shed light on the creative process in artists like Kafka, van Gogh, and Beethoven by revealing their personal conflicts and claiming that these found expression in their art. Shrill cries of dismay were expressed. "How does this help me appreciate the power of Beethoven's music, the beauty of Vincent's paintings, the profundity of Kafka's stories? Who cares if a composer has a paranoid streak, if a painter is self-destructive, if a writer is suffering from a guilt complex?"

To the extent that the psychologists in question simply showed how their subjects were sick, I would join in the chorus of protests. To the extent, too, that their revelations amounted to nothing more than gossip about the great, I would be glad to see them discredited. When the psychobiographer's aim is not, however, to reveal pathology or dig up some dirt, but rather to essay the task of demonstrating the subtle relations between a creative individual's personality, process of growth, and creative accomplishments, I see no reason to object.

Quite the contrary. The aim of such studies is not primarily to elucidate the work of the person in question. It is to elucidate the creative process—and if this process is shown to operate superbly in otherwise fallible human beings, if, in fact, the process is shown to arise out of their very fallibility, so much the better for our understanding of the wondrousness of human nature. Far from degrading the creative artist, the psychobiographer who does the job well expands our appreciation of the artist's achievement, by showing us the pain and confusion out of which beauty and truth may be wrested and held aloft. As William Styron has his painter say in *Lie Down in Darkness,* "I will squeeze this until beauty runs out of it."

As far as the present study is concerned, what I intend to do is train the searchlight of the psychobiographer on a set of psychologists themselves. But why, you may ask, do I wish to do it. What is *my* motivation for examining the motivations of the leaders of my field? I suspect there are many intertwining factors and to pursue them all might strain your patience. Let me tell just one of the things I know of myself, therefore, and let you speculate about the rest to the extent of your interest.

Skepticism, doubt, or incredulity are clearly at the heart of my enterprise. Why are these qualities important to me? I have already said that I discovered in early adulthood that I was not a true believer. When I think back to my childhood, however, I see that the seeds of doubt were instilled in me very early. I grew up as a middle-class Jewish boy in Winnipeg in the 1930s and 1940s. As a member of a minority group on the rise in that society, as a member, too, of a small country caught between the giants of Great Britain and the United States, it was common to be skeptical of all claims to greatness and infallibility. Those who held power, we little people thought, were too often pompous and self-righteous. While we were unable to depose them, we could at least see their moral failings.

At the same time, within my immediate family, my father stood for belief in traditional Jewish doctrine while my mother fried bacon for breakfast and represented a more modern attitude. I was wholly identified with my mother. She was the one I loved, the one who constituted my security, and I adopted her outlook on life more readily than that of my father. Her family too—my one aunt and several uncles—were all something less than true believers (one of my uncles, indeed, often preached that all men were corrupt, and he should have known, since he spent many years in prison), though they paid lip service to the rituals my grandparents cherished; and I think my closeness to them bolstered my emerging skepticism.

By the time I was an adolescent, I took pride in writing humorous pieces in which I made fun of all pretensions, all claims to greatness and The Truth. At my high school graduation I presented a comic skit that so ridiculed the office of valedictorian that the real valedictorian broke into tears—over which I felt guilty for years.

It is clear, therefore, that my incentive for writing a book on the fallibility of the leaders of my field is as much a continuation of my lifelong pattern of incredulity as of any intention to communicate a truth I can claim as my own. I do not deny it. When I quit the Jung Institute in my twenties, I was accused of being rebelliously adolescent. Perhaps I was; perhaps I still am. The question, I think, is not how we label the source of my motivation, but what I can make of it. Given my propensity for skepticism, how effectively can I use it to elucidate the making of psychology?

Putting it that way, however, I realize that I am straying dangerously close to the position of those who oppose psychobiography. Lest I go too far, therefore, and lend power to my opponents (why should I be so good to them?), I want to draw this confession to a close in the hope that seeing a bit of my psychodynamics will not deter you from accompanying me in my effort to expose the problems of psychology and its leaders.

I have chosen to present my case by focusing first on two pioneers, Wilhelm Wundt and William James; then discussing personality theory as a projection of the theorist's personality traits; then showing how psychotherapy is an art form rather than a science, which makes it more or less a projection of the therapist's characteristics, too; and finally portraying psychology as an all-too-human undertaking, an assessment that should lead us to accept the principles and proposals of the field with more than a few grains of salt.

In the course of this presentation, I examine the lives and works of five men who were arguably the greatest psychologists of all—Freud, Jung, Skinner, Rogers, and Erickson—showing in each case how the man's contributions represented his own needs, traits, and preoccupations. My purpose in beginning with Wundt and James is to demonstrate that from the very start there were diametrically opposed ways of operating within the discipline, diametrically opposed convictions on how to study human nature, and—my major point—diametrically opposed conceptions of the mind, reflecting the minds that conceived them more directly than the Mind, if there is such a thing, of the typical human being.

From start to finish, other leaders could have been selected, and I regret that I have not included any women. I wrestled with this decision for some time, consulted colleagues of both sexes, and reluctantly came to the conclusion that psychology does not have female pioneers of the stature of the men I have chosen. Critics may call this a sexist interpretation on my part; I think it simply illustrates the traditional sexism of the field. Women, I have no doubt, are as astute as men in understanding personality and equally gifted in the practice of psychotherapy. In the formation of the field, however, they did not have the opportunity to demonstrate outstanding leadership.

In any case, I hope you will agree that the men I discuss were significant enough in the history of psychology to warrant my focus on them alone. My selection of subjects, however, is not the primary issue; my thesis is. If I can demonstrate that psychology is made in the image of its makers, then the validity of the theories and techniques of the field would have to be seen as highly relative, and true believers of any stripe would have to give way to the advent of eclecticism. And that, I contend, is as it must be, for in the hundred-odd years of its existence, not one of the schools of thought that have dominated the discipline has ever proved applicable to more than a portion of human experience.

# 3

# The Forerunners
## Wundt and James

## AT THE OUTSET: PSYCHOLOGY IN TWO PERSPECTIVES

Wilhelm Wundt and William James, the German William and the American, formed a perfect set of opposites in kicking off the brand new field of psychology. In their personal traits as well as in their outlooks on the mind, they were as different as two men of the nineteenth century could be. Wundt was a model of precision and control, while James was high-strung, ebullient, and unrestrained. Wundt embodied the exactitude and authoritarianism that were characteristic of the Prussian society in which he was raised, while James observed that Wundt's psychology "could not have arisen in any country where the inhabitants had the capacity to be bored."

Wundt's method of studying mental processes was precise and rigid, a lockstep approach designed to unearth the so-called elements of consciousness, or the bits and pieces that fused to form ideas and trains of thought. A description by a contemporary gives an impression of the man. "Wundt would appear (in the classroom) at exactly the correct minute—punctuality was essential—dressed all in black and carrying a small sheaf of lecture notes. He clattered up the side aisle to the platform with an awkward shuffle as if his soles were made of wood. On the platform was a long desk where demonstrations were performed. He made a few gestures—a forefinger across his forehead, a rearrangement of his chalk—then faced his audience and placed his elbows on the bookrest. His voice was weak at first, then gained in strength and emphasis. As he talked, his arms and hands moved up and down, pointing and waving, in some mysterious way illustrative. His head and body were rigid and only the hands played back and forth . . . As the clock struck the end of the hour he stopped and, stooping a little, clattered out as he had clattered in" (Miller & Buckhout, 1973, p. 27).

James was Wundt's foremost opponent. He proclaimed that there were no "elements of consciousness," no bits and pieces worth investigating, for the mind was a process, not a thing, a welter of impressions, feelings, and ideas in flux, best described as "the stream of consciousness."

In contrast to the European whose stance was so stiff and formal, the American's teaching style was uninhibited in the extreme. A spare, wiry man, energetic and colorful, he would stretch himself out on the floor to make a point and was so fond of humorous observations that a student once chastised him with, "Professor James, to be serious for *just* a moment . . ." Original concepts, arresting images, and homely illustrations poured out of him in profusion.

Describing the controlling power of habits, for instance, he wrote, "The marksman sees the bird and before he knows it, he has aimed and shot. A gleam in his adversary's eye, a momentary pressure from his rapier, and the fencer finds that he has instantly made the right parry and return. A glance at the musical hieroglyphics, and the pianist's fingers have rippled through a shower of notes . . . which way does my door swing? I cannot tell the answer; yet my hand never makes a mistake" (James, 1961, pp. 6–7). And of his rival's ideas, he declared, "(Wundt's) psychology talks like one who would say that a river consists of nothing but pailsful, spoonsful, quartpotsful, barrelsful, and other moulded forms of water. Even were the pails and pots all actually standing in the stream, still between them the free water would continue to flow" (p. 32).

But why am I telling you these stories? What purpose do I have in evoking these figures of the past? Do I suppose you have much interest in Wundt or James, or much to learn from their teachings? Probably not. My goal lies in another direction. What I hope to show is that, from the very start, psychology has been made in the images of its makers, that the leaders of the field have quite unwittingly assumed that the human mind must be like their own minds, that human nature must conform to their own personality traits. My accounts of the two Williams are intended as a prologue to my work, like the opening movement of a symphony in which the themes to be developed are introduced.

Quite simply, then, I would like to show you how Wilhelm Wundt grew up to become a stiff, formal character, a man of unflagging zeal but little spontaneity, and how these characteristics both enabled him to initiate a scientific approach to the mind, yet led him to adopt a conception of the mind that would ultimately prove sterile; and I would like to show how William James grew up to become a colorful, loquacious character, given to moods of despair and flights of inspiration, how he was particularly open to the spiritual dimension of life, while closed to the sexual dimension, and how these characteristics determined his view of the mind as a flowing stream, enabled him brilliantly to explore the psychology of religion, but kept him shy of the kinds of insights Freud was producing at the time.

In sum, I intend to show how Wundt's and James's personal selves determined the contributions they made to psychology, and how their guiding images of the mind were essentially images of their own minds. Great men they were, no doubt about it, but locked into themselves nonetheless. Locked into themselves and into their surroundings, for neither they nor any of the other psychologists we will discuss grew up in a cultural vacuum. Their outlooks and values were colored by the times and places in which they lived; so I will also provide perspectives on their environments. The end I am aiming for in each case is an evolving portrait of a leader of psychology, the way he became the kind of person he was, and the ways in which his characteristics gave direction to his leadership within the field.

## THE WORLD OF WILHELM WUNDT: A SYSTEM OF BUILDING BLOCKS

The time is 1875. The German Empire, whose fortunes have been directed for a dozen years by Otto von Bismarck, has become the most powerful nation on the Continent. Her population will increase by 20 million in the next two generations and she already leads the world in industrial chemistry. Her scientists are renowned, especially in physiology, where men like Johannes Müller and Hermann von Helmholz have earned distinguished reputations, while Ernst Weber and Gustav Fechner have explored a new area of inquiry called psychophysics, whose aim is no less than to measure the precise relationship between the physical world and the mind of man.

This is the "age of expansion," the onset of the industrial revolution. Throughout Europe, science has established itself as the architect of progress and is fast replacing poetry, philosophy, and religion as the ultimate source of truth. The first World's Fair was held in England in 1851. An ocean cable has linked Britain and the United States since 1866. The Suez Canal was completed by the French in 1869. The typewriter was invented in 1874 and the telephone will be in use from 1876. Synthetic dyes will soon transform the fabric industries, synthetic medicines and fertilizers are being developed, and refrigeration is not far off. With increased urbanization, popular education is becoming feasible, food is more plentiful than ever before, and clothing and housing are being improved every day. Yet the personal gap between employer and employee is rapidly widening, the average citizen is still a pawn to his country's rulers, and in Germany—as in France, Britain, Russia, and Austria—pompous, power-seeking monarchy prevails. The image of Bismarck, stern autocrat, all-powerful and intolerant, reflects an ideal of German fathers throughout the nation, an ideal that is to have a profound effect on the founder of *Psychologie*.

The place we are interested in, amid all the panoply of empire and cacophony of industrialization, is the city of Leipzig, not far from the border of Czechoslovakia in what is now known as East Germany. Its renowned university, at which Goethe himself had been a student about a hundred years earlier, is in process of allowing one of its recently appointed professors to establish something new in the world—a laboratory for the scientific study of the mind.

The professor's name is Wilhelm Wundt. He is forty-three years old and has accepted a chair of philosophy at the venerable institution, though his field of greatest expertise is physiology. This confluence of philosophy and physiology giving rise to psychology is understandable, for it stands to reason that scholars conversant with the study of thought and the study of the brain would gravitate toward a specialty whose focus is the mind.

What brings Wundt to this focus, however, and what will determine the kind of contribution he is to make to this uncharted domain? These are the questions we must pursue. If we examine his upbringing and salient personality traits, we will soon arrive at an answer.

Wundt was born in 1832 at Neckarau, a suburb of Mannheim. He was the youngest of four children, but only he and one brother survived the years of childhood. Wilhelm's father performed the duties of a country parson. Generous to a fault, he allowed his parishioners to take advantage of him; and his wife to control the family's finances. Not only their finances; Frau Wundt and her relatives controlled the raising of the children as well, and Wilhelm was well into adulthood and had been thoroughly indoctrinated with their habits and values before he escaped their direct influence.

Frau Wundt was strict and demanding, a humorless woman who rarely expressed affection. Her father, whose home the boy visited regularly, was also a petty tyrant. In the spirit of Bismarck, he was, in Wundt's words, "a man of the greatest precision," who frowned upon the slightest deviation from the schedule of household routine. Discipline at his hands was inflexible, and Wundt later recalled his terror at being confined to dark closets as punishment for minor infractions.

Wilhelm became a deeply introverted youngster. His only friend was a retarded boy a few years older, and the only adult he felt close to was his tutor. He indulged in endless daydreams and it was said that "although he loved his tutor, he loved his fantasies more." When the man moved to another village, his absence produced such severe depression in the boy that he was allowed to live with him for a year before entering *gymnasium*.

At the boarding school to which he was sent, Wilhelm was timid and withdrawn. Instead of playing with the other boys or devoting himself to his studies, he spent so much time in his dream world that he was finally allowed to join his brother at an aunt's home and attend the same school as he.

At nineteen, the young man entered the university, but like so many young men before and since, he was not yet sure what he wanted to study. His father had died and his mother was living on a meager pension. His scholastic record had been only mediocre, so he did not qualify for state aid. One of his maternal uncles, however, convinced him to study cerebral anatomy, and the mysteries of the brain soon captivated him completely. "Suddenly," according to one of his biographers, "he had become the industrious, seemingly indefatigable Wundt who would be so astonishingly productive in future years" (Diamond, 1980, p. 17).

The astonishing productivity to which his biographer refers became legendary even within Wundt's lifetime. This man who had started his academic career so hesitantly, who as a child was withdrawn and incapable of scholastic success, was to publish almost 500 articles and books, totaling close to 60,000 printed pages, while single-handedly establishing the discipline of experimental psychology.

As a subsequent events were to prove, Wundt was an outstanding organizer. Like his grandfather before him, he became "a man of the greatest precision," a systematizer and classifier of knowledge. He held that psychology is *Erfahrungswissenschaft*, the science of conscious experience, and the method of investigation he employed was known as "controlled introspection." For Wundt, introspection was not a matter of wondering about oneself, but a disciplined mental exercise in separating simple experiences into their basic elements. If you were a subject in one of his experiments, here is what might have happened.

"Professor Wundt holds up a pencil and asks you what you see. 'A pencil,' you proudly reply. 'No,' he admonishes, waving the object in front of your face. 'You do not see a pencil. That is an idea you have formed. What do you actually see?" Gradually getting the point, you tell him you see a long, narrow, yellow object sharpened at one end with a black tip, and with something that seems softer and pinkish at the other end. The professor smiles, for he has gotten across his view that even such a common thing as a pencil is a complex idea made up of a combination of simpler sensations" (Mindess & Munford, 1979, p. 224–5).

Wundt's approach to the mind bore a strong resemblance to what was occurring at the time in chemistry. Just as Germany's chemists had contributed to the establishment of the Table of Elements—the molecular building blocks of the physical world—he hoped to establish a kind of table of mental elements that would constitute the building blocks of the psychological world. It was a hope that was doomed to defeat, but it inspired a good deal of the activity in his Leipzig lab.

Perhaps the most provocative of all Wundt's experiments and theories, or at least the ones that most clearly exposed the limitations of his approach, were those in which he attempted to analyze feelings. Using himself as his only subject, he listened for hours to a metronome, varying the speed of the clicks and noting his sensations as he awaited each successive sound. Mild tension and relief, mild pleasure and displeasure were what he experienced. As a result, he eventually held that *all* feelings—love, hate, joy, grief, and so on—could be adequately described as combinations of certain degrees of agreeableness or disagreeableness, strain or relaxation, and excitement or calm.

From the vantage point of anyone who is not a devout Wundtian, it must seem that such an approach is monumentally irrelevant. Granted the ingenuity of focusing on a simple event like listening to a metronome, granted the boldness of trying to discover the basic structure of feeling, still the experimental procedure is so far removed from anything truly emotional that one gets the impression of a scientist attempting to explain the surge of the sea by shaking a test tube of water and noting the undulations of the liquid.

While it may seem degrading to Wundt's genius to call him a compulsive personality (today's term for what used to be called an obsessive-compulsive character), there can be little doubt that such traits were predominant in his personality. Not only do his experiments support this interpretation, but his prodigious writings, so heavy with supplementary clauses that by the time one gets to the end of a sentence one has forgotten how it began, provide further evidence. These observations should not be taken to indicate that Wundt was an unpleasant man. On the contrary, he was unfailingly patient, courteous, and helpful to those with whom he worked. The qualities he lacked were spontaneity, warmth, and humor. He had so fully incorporated the values of his family and his culture that his entire adult life was dominated by the drive to produce—in his case, to produce meticulous, intellectualized accounts of everyday human experience.

From the perspective of our time and place, Wundt's personality may seem neurotic. It would be easy for us to write him off as a product of repressive Prussian society and his family's unhealthy influence. We may assume that the withdrawn young man who lived in his dream world was drawn to psychology by a need to probe his own mental processes and that his circumstantial approach was dictated by his compulsive temperament. These conclusions would not be unwarranted except for the fact that Wundt was not neurotic in the sense of being unhappy, confused, or incapable of exercising his abilities. Quite the contrary: what he did was to capitalize on his character traits by finding a way to use them to advantage. Compulsiveness, we must conclude, may be less an infirmity than a way of being. While blocking one's ability to enjoy life's pleasures and interfering with the experience of love and passion, such a temperament may enable a person to accomplish wondrous feats—to construct intricate systems and devices, to come close to perfection in his work or, in Wundt's case, to establish a brand-new area of scientific investigation.

Being locked into one's self, therefore, is not necessarily the imprisonment it may seem, for out of one's own resources—out of one's neurotic propensities, in fact—one may fashion things of beauty and value. Wundt's personal characteristics limited his understanding of the mind, for he was compelled to see it only as a system of building blocks, a view that rigidifies its functions and fails to accord it sufficient freedom. Ironically, however, these very characteristics enabled him to achieve what he did. Growing up in a society in which scientific accomplishments were accorded the highest value, temperamentally attuned to the spirit that prevailed, he established the scientific method as a viable approach to the mind, and on that ground alone his legitimate claim to greatness endures.

## William James: A Flowing Stream

William James was a different sort of person entirely. Born and raised in New York in the 1840s and 50s (he was ten years younger than Wundt), he grew up in a household as different from the German professor's as spring is from the dead of winter. William's father, independently wealthy, was an idealist, a socialist, a religious philosopher, and an astonishingly permissive man who expressed his love for his family with unstinting abundance. Affectionate phrases like, "My lovely boys," "my darlings," "the light of my life," and, "words can't tell how dear you are to my heart," were always on his lips. He also encouraged his children to share his enthusiasm for intellectual debate. From their earliest years, their opinions were solicited and received with interest.

As a result, wrote one of their many friends, "Within that family circle, nothing . . . was ever stagnant. The father led them into fields of conversation of the widest possible range, and conflicting ideas flourished with intensity and ardor. . . . There could not be a more entertaining treat than a dinner at the James house when all the young people were at home. They were full of stories of the oddest kind, and discussed questions of morals or taste or literature with a vociferous vigor so great as sometimes to lead the young men to leave their seats and gesticulate on the floor" (Matthiessen, 1947, p. 71).

The indulgent atmosphere of the James house was hardly typical of the day, but mid-nineteenth century New York was much more likely to produce the intellectual ferment of that home than the Prussian society of Wundt. By 1859, the city had become the nation's chief seaport, and more than 100 steamers were carrying passengers up the Hudson to Albany. By 1860, almost all the heavily populated sections of New York State had railroad service, while its massive lumber industry was making fortunes for many. The garment trade, meanwhile, was providing employment—under dreadful working conditions, unfortunately—for thousands of immigrants in the city. Poles, Irish, and Germans were arriving in droves, and by the mid-1860s, when William was in his twenties, over 300,000 were living in the slums.

Yet wondrously beautiful Central Park had been built at a cost of millions and was available to all, art and literature flourished, and the metropolis was fast becoming what it was to remain—the cultural heart of the nation. William Cullen Bryant, Horace Greeley, Edgar Allan Poe, Walt Whitman, Ralph Waldo Emerson, Herman Melville, and other literary figures spent goodly parts of their lives in New York City.

New York State, meanwhile, was alive with religious fervor. Revivalist meetings were popular; Joseph Smith founded the Church of Jesus Christ of Latter-Day Saints in an upstate community. John Henry Noyes, reacting against the prevailing Calvinism that William's father would also reject, formed a society in Putney, Vermont, known as the "Bible Communists" that practiced free love; but when he was arrested on charges of adultery, fled to Oneida in Central New York and established the Oneida Community, one of the most successful Utopian experiments in America.

William Miller attracted thousands to his tent meetings in Rochester, even after his predictions of the end of the world failed to materialize; and in the 1850s an assortment of groups known as "Spiritualists" claimed a million converts throughout the world, one-third of them living in New York State. The first women's rights convention was held in Seneca Falls in 1848, and the state was alive with concern over abolition and temperance when the Civil War broke out in 1861. The Southern attack on Fort Sumter brought New York into the Union cause, but as a result of fiery opposition to conscription, a riot in the city left almost 1000 dead in the very first year of the conflict.

By the time the war ended in 1865, when William was twenty-three and still far from finding his calling, New York had entered a new economic era. It had firmly established itself as the urban industrial hub of this country, as well as its cultural center, the largest and most exciting city in America for generations yet to come. Its throbbing vitality enveloped the James's home in William's youth, and while he was shielded from its coarser elements by his father's wealth and sensitivity, and though he was also exposed to years of European education and travel, some of his intensity and alertness must have been reinforced by the milieu in which he spent his formative years.

In any case, two of the offspring of the James family grew

up to be geniuses—Henry, the famous novelist; and the subject of our study, William. Before William decided to devote himself to psychology, however, he was to endure both doubt and despair, as well as exhibiting a host of psychosomatic and psychoneurotic symptoms. The remarkably liberated atmosphere of his home, it seems, not only kindled his intellectual curiosity, but also left him awash in the limitless possibilities of life. He attended numerous schools, spent years in Germany, France, and Switzerland, eventually enrolled at Harvard, but by his late twenties had studied painting, chemistry, medicine, physiology, and botany without committing himself to a career in any one of these fields. His indecision produced depression.

At one point he wrote home from Berlin, "My habits of mind have been so bad that I feel as if the greater part of the last ten years had been worse than wasted, and now have so little surplus of physical vigor as to shrink from trying to retrieve them. Too late! Too late!" Again, "I confess that, in the lonesome gloom which beset me for a couple of months last summer, the only feeling that kept me from giving up was that by waiting and living, by hook or crook, long enough, I might make my *nick*, however small a one, in the raw stuff the race has had to shape, and so assert my reality" (Matthiessen, 1947, p. 215). At other times, he complained about a sense of despair contaminated with physical ailments including back trouble, eye trouble, indigestion, and insomnia. These years of unhappiness, however, culminated in a crisis that was to prove the turning point of his life.

William's father was a Swedenborgian. He had adopted the Swedish mystic's spiritualism as the result of an experience (he called it a "vastation") he had had in his thirties that we would now call "an existential crisis." This event—a sudden realization of the reality of evil—had caused him years of anxiety, until he put his soul to rest in the teachings of Swedenborg.

William, his father's son in this as in many ways, underwent a similar experience when he was close to thirty. As he later wrote,

> Whilst in this state of philosophic pessimism and general depression of spirits . . . I went one evening into a dressing-room in the twilight . . . when suddenly there fell upon me without any warning,

just as if it came out of the darkness, a horrible fear of my own existence. Simultaneously there arose in my mind the image of an epileptic patient whom I had seen in the asylum, a black-haired youth with greenish skin, entirely idiotic, who used to sit all day on one of the benches . . . with his knees drawn up against his chin, and the coarse gray undershirt, which was his only garment, drawn over them inclosing the entire figure. He sat there like a sculptured Egyptian cat or Peruvian mummy, moving nothing but his black eyes and looking absolutely non-human. This image and my fear entered into a species of combination with each other. *That shape am I,* I felt, potentially. Nothing that I possess can defend me against that fate, if the hour for it should strike for me as it struck for him. There was such a horror of him, and such a perception of my own merely momentary discrepancy from him, that it was as if something hitherto solid within my breast gave way entirely, and I became a mass of quivering fear. After this the universe was changed for me altogether. I awoke morning after morning with a horrible dread at the pit of my stomach, and with a sense of the insecurity of life that I never knew before, and that I have never felt since. It was like a revelation; and although the immediate feelings passed away, the experience has made me sympathetic with the morbid feelings of others ever since. It gradually faded, but for months I was unable to go out into the dark alone." (James, 1902, p. 157–8)

Considering the intensity of his despair, it is all the more striking that, without the help of any sort of psychotherapist, he eventually fought his way clear. What started him on his path of redemption was a philosophic challenge to his will. In his diary, he wrote, "I think that yesterday was a crisis in my life. I finished the first part of (the French philosopher) Renouvier's second 'Essais' and see no reason why his definition of Free Will—'the sustaining of a thought *because I choose to* when I might have other thoughts'—need be the definition of an illusion. At any rate, I will assume for the present—until next year—that it is no illusion. *My first act of free will shall be to believe in free will* (italics mine) . . . Hitherto, when I have felt like taking a free initiative, like daring to act originally . . . suicide seemed the most manly form to put my daring into; now, I will go a step farther with my will, not only act with it, but believe as well; believe in my individual reality and creative power . . . Life shall (be built in) doing and suffering and creating" (Matthiessen 1947, p. 218).

The significance of this turning point cannot be overemphasized. Renouvier's assertion of the reality of free will gave William the opportunity to believe in his own ability to raise himself up by his bootstraps, shake off his physical infirmities and philosophic doubts, and declare, not as Descartes had done centuries earlier, "I think, therefore I am," but, "I am, therefore I will be."

William grasped that opportunity, soon returned to America, and within two years had accepted a position as instructor of anatomy and physiology at Harvard. He wrote his brother Henry, "The appointment to teach physiology is a perfect godsend to me just now. An external motive to work, which yet does not strain me, a dealing with men instead of my own mind, and a diversion from those introspective studies which had bred a sort of philosophical hypochondria in me of late and which it will certainly do me good to drop for a year" (p. 219).

The following winter, their father wrote Henry, "Willy goes on swimmingly with his teaching. His students (fifty-seven) are elated with their luck in having such a professor, and next year he will have no doubt a larger class still. . . . He came in here the other afternoon when I was sitting alone, and after walking the floor in an animated way for a moment, exclaimed, 'Dear me! what a difference there is between me now and me last spring this time; then so hypochondriacal . . . and now feeling my mind so cleared up and restored to sanity. It is the difference between death and life.'. . . I ventured to ask what specially in his opinion had promoted the change. He said several things: the reading of Renouvier . . . and Wordsworth . . . but especially his having given up the notion that all mental disorder required to have a physical basis. This had become perfectly untrue to him. He saw that the mind did act irrespectively of material coercion, and could be dealt with therefore at first-hand, and this was health to his bones" (p. 219).

William's grappling with the nature of the mind was part of his successful struggle to restore his own well-being. As if to confirm the step he had taken, he created a course at Harvard entitled,

"The Relations Between Physiology and Psychology." He was then thirty-three. At the age of thirty-six, he married Alice Gibbons, a young woman to whom he had been introduced by his father. In the same year, 1878, he agreed to write a psychology textbook for Henry Holt and Company, apologetically estimating that it might take him as long as 2 years to complete it. It took him 12, but when *The Principles of Psychology* appeared in 1890, one of the most brilliant minds in the history of the field had declared itself.

Familiarly known as "The James," *The Principles* was followed by a briefer version nicknamed "The Jimmy." William's colorful style enlivened his subject matter so vividly that he was chastised by critics for failing to maintain a somber enough approach. A more understanding judge, however, later said, "The power of his mind lay in its extreme mobility, its darting, exploratory impulsiveness. It was not a mind which remained stationary, drawing all things to itself as a centre, but a mind which traveled widely—now here and now there—seeing all things for itself, and making up in the variety of its adventures for what it lacked in poise" (Perry, 1935, p. 206).

In a key chapter called "The Stream of Consciousness," James wrote, "Consciousness . . . is nothing jointed; it flows. A river or a stream are the metaphors by which it is most naturally described. In talking of it hereafter, let us call it the stream of thought, of consciousness, or of subjective life." The essence of this image, clearly, is the notion that the mind must be seen as *fluid*, as alive and moving, forever changing and doing, not simply recording images but actively organizing its impressions and creating new ideas.

Central to James's contribution to psychology, the image is also central to James himself. *His mind,* it should be apparent, was just such a lively stream. His entire upbringing had produced a man who was the very embodiment of his teaching. As the exceptionally formal, rigid Wundt was compelled to see the mind as a structure of building blocks that could be neatly catalogued, the exceptionally informal, fluid James was destined to see it as a flowing stream. The point is not who was right or wrong, nor even which concept we may prefer. What I am trying to make clear is the fact that these early psychologists' teachings were extensions of themselves, projections of their own experience upon the enigma of human nature.

James's contribution did not end with *The Principles of Psychology*. He developed a number of original theories, and in 1902 published a series of lectures he had delivered at Edinburgh entitled, *The Varieties of Religious Experience*. Widely read and admired to this day, *The Varieties* is a thoroughly engrossing work. What William set out to do was "first, to defend *experience* against *philosophy* as being the real backbone of the world's religious life . . . and second, to make the hearer or reader believe, what I myself invincibly do believe, that although all the special manifestations of religion may have been absurd (I mean its creeds and theories), yet the life of it as a whole is mankind's most important function" (Perry, vol. II, pp. 326–7). Religious feeling and belief, he argued, are profound parts of human nature. They take many forms, both beautiful and grotesque, and serve many functions, both wondrous and banal. If we are students of humanity, we must attempt to understand religious cravings, convictions, and delusions, for they may be the very ore from which the human soul is mined.

James was well equipped for this task. Not only had his father been preoccupied with religious questions and studied them seriously, but Ralph Waldo Emerson, the leading religious philosopher of the day, had been a friend of the family when William was a child. More to the point of our inquiry, however, is a curious fact reported by his brother Henry. Reminiscing about their childhood, Henry wrote,

> Our young liberty in respect to church-going was absolute and we might range at will, through the great city, from one place of worship and one form of faith to another, or might on occasion ignore them all equally, which was what we mainly did . . . Going forth hand in hand into the sunshine . . . we sampled, in modern phrase, as small unprejudiced inquirers obeying their inspiration, any resort of any congregation detected by us . . ." What church do you go to?"—the challenge took in childish circles that searching form; of the form it took among our elders my impression is more vague . . . It was colder than any criticism, I recall, to hear our father reply that we could plead nothing less than the whole privilege of Christendom and that there was no communion, even that of

the Catholics, even that of the Jews, even that of the Swedenbor-
gians, from which we need find ourselves excluded. (Matthiessen,
1947, pp. 82–3)

The James children, in other words, attended every church
they could find, their father insisting all the while that religious
experience was a wonderful thing and one should be open to the
teachings of every creed. How fitting, then, that one of these children—the one, indeed, who was so much his father's son—should
write *The Varieties of Religious Experience,* a book in which religious experience is presented as wonderful, but no one religion
is extolled over all the others. Not only must we agree that the
child is father to the man, but also that the man in his maturity
grapples with issues bequeathed by his early experience and, in
resolving them, affirms himself while contributing the fruits of his
labors to the world.

The most profound tie in William's life was his relation to
his father. When the old man lay on his deathbed, William, then
in London, wrote

Darling old Father . . . We have been so long accustomed to the
hypothesis of you being taken away from us . . . that the thought
that this may be your last illness conveys no very sudden shock.
You are old enough, you've given your message to the world in
many ways and will not be forgotten; you are left alone, and on
the other side, let us hope and pray, dear, dear old Mother is waiting
for you to join her . . . Meanwhile, my blessed old Father, I scribble
this line just to tell you how full of the tenderest memories and
feelings about you my heart has for the last few days been filled.
In that mysterious gulf of the past into which the present soon will
fall, yours is still for me the central figure. All my intellectual life
I derive from you; and though we have often seemed at odds in
the expression thereof, I'm sure there's a harmony somewhere,
and that our strivings will combine. What my debt to you is goes
beyond all my power of estimating—so early, so penetrating, and
so constant has been the influence . . . It comes strangely over me
in bidding you good-bye how a life is but a day and expresses but
a single note. It is so much like the act of bidding an ordinary good-
night. Good-night, my sacred old Father! If I don't see you again—
Farewell! a blessed farewell! Your William.'' (Matthiessen, 1947,
p. 132)

*The Varieties of Religious Experience,* William's final masterpiece, was a tribute to this man who had so richly nourished his son's mind and heart. The psychologist's genius, we may say, was fostered by his father's encouragement and example, and his great work was in a sense a culmination of his father's commitment to the religious spirit.

William's upbringing, however, was not as entirely idyllic as it may seem. We have already seen how the freedom of opportunity he was afforded left him for a time unable to decide what to do with his life; but more important to his view of man is the fact that there was one subject that was *not* open to debate in the family circle. That subject was sex. As Jean Strouse (1980) writes in her biography of William's sister Alice, "Sex was not a topic of discussion in the James household. William disliked the word all his life. He rarely mentioned sex in all his work on psychology and religious experience, but in . . . the second volume of *The Principles of Psychology,* he posited, under the heading 'love,' an *anti-sexual instinct'* . . . the actual repulsiveness to us of the idea of intimate contact with most of the persons we meet, especially those of our own sex' " (p. 54).

It is practically certain that William remained a virgin until his marriage at age thirty-six. As far as we know, he enjoyed a satisfactory relationship with his wife, and they did have a number of children. Nevertheless, his character was so firmly fashioned by the Puritan morality of the time, he was so much the product of New England society and the intellectual-religious atmosphere of his home, that all the vagaries of lust and sensuality remained outside his pale. He denied himself not only the freedom to taste their delights, but even the liberty to contemplate their part in life. While Freud, therefore, in the very years when James was coming into his own, was developing his sexual theories in the cosmopolitan, libertine atmosphere of *fin de siècle* Vienna, James was writing marvellous works on religion and the mind while recoiling from examination of the earthier aspects of human nature. As a result, his distinctive contribution to psychology was, in the words of Gordon Allport, "old-fashioned" and "perhaps even a bit pious."

Jamesian man, to sum up, was a God-seeking, asexual creature, one with a free-flowing mind, gentle and passionate feelings, but few lustful cravings worth noting. He was a thing of habit, but possessed of free will nonetheless, an impressionable, vital being fascinated by the multiplicity of life. The image, it should be clear, is (especially with regard to sex) more consonant with the character of its author than with that of humanity at large. Nevertheless—and despite its one glaring fault—it is an exciting image, as inspiring as the man who gave it form.

## "THE ELEMENTS" VERSUS "THE STREAM:" AN AUGURY OF THE FORKS OF THE FUTURE

To recall that that man had been ready to commit suicide before he found the will to complete his work on earth is to be awed by the life-and-death struggles that may underlie a person's fulfillment of his potentials. At the same time, to set James's view of the mind against Wundt's—the "*stream* of consciousness" versus the "*elements* of consciousness"—is to portray the first of the innumerable rifts that were to turn psychology into the unceasing debating-ground it is to this day.

I trust I have made it clear that their basic views were determined by their central character traits. What I have not yet dwelt on, but will in chapters to come, are the ways in which this projection of the psychologist's characteristics onto the human race helps the leaders of the field affirm themselves as individuals.

# 4

# Personality Theory as an Inkblot

## The Source of All Personality Theories: Their Authors' Traits

Personality theorists do not set out to create theories of personality. They simply go about their business, treating patients, teaching students, writing books, and living their lives. As observers of the human scene, they take note of the characteristics of the people with whom they come in contact, and as introspective individuals, they dwell on their own thoughts and feelings. Eventually, however, they become intrigued by the possibility of making sense of it all. Commonly presaged by a period of personal dissatisfaction, by confusion over their own needs and aspirations, they seek intellectual clarity. In this groping state, they begin to formulate hypotheses. Freud's concept of the Oedipus complex, Jung's introversion-extroversion, Adler's notion of inferiority-superiority dynamics, Maslow's drive for self-actualization, were all attempts to extend their observations of the people they knew, and especially of the one person each of them was most concerned with, into principles applicable to the human race.

The hypotheses each theorist puts forth, in short, are derivatives of his own experience, understandable though unadmitted inferences that all other persons are like the persons he has happened to observe, and particularly like the person he has observed most of all. The enigma of human nature, we may say, is like a giant Rorschach blot onto which each personality theorist projects his own personality characteristics.

Two brilliant psychologists, Clyde Kluckhohn and Henry Murray, once summed up the essential facts from which personality theory takes off by stating that in some respects every person is like all other persons, in some respects like some other persons, and in some respects like no other person. In what respects, however, are we all alike and what makes us differ when we do? If we can be clustered into groups sharing similar traits, what makes us fall into one or another group? Are the forces that shape us primarily genetic or environmental? Are they behavioral, emotional, cognitive, or spiritual? How much of what we become as adults is set down in early childhood? How much can be changed and, where change is possible, how can we improve the characteristics with which we began?

All personality theorists have views on these matters. Their commitment to their views, moreover, is remarkable for its unshakability. Especially the theorists who are considered great, the truly creative contributors to the field, invariably defend their ideas with vigor and, having enunciated them, cling to them for the rest of their lives. Their concepts are not, to their minds at least, merely propositions that may shed some light in the darkness, but Revealed Truth.

Do I state my case too strongly? I can claim good company, for both Freud and Jung—the men I am about to use as prime examples—were nothing if not adamantine in their faith in their own theories. Freud withstood widespread criticism for decades, first from the philistines who found his emphasis on sexuality perverse[1], then from his former disciples, and never wavered in the least. Jung, for whom spirituality and ancient beliefs were major concerns, went from the study of the occult to the study of mythology to the study of alchemy, while his more conventional colleagues shook their heads at his increasing obscurantism.

The essential point for us to note is that no one becomes engaged in explaining personality before he has a personality of his own. The personality of the theorist, furthermore, must be an important reference point in judging the validity of his theoretical propositions. If an idea does not jibe with my experience of myself, how can I accept it it as applying to the human race? If it does, on the other hand, throw light on my personal experience, how can I help but believe in its explanatory power? Indeed, if the idea is enlightening enough, if it not only helps me understand myself in an abstract sense but also enables me to overcome confusion or despair, how can I not want to preach it to the world?

In *The Place of the Sciences of Man in the System of Sciences,* Jean Piaget (1970) wrote, "The two most ready tendencies of spontaneous thought . . . are to assume that one stands at the center of the world, both spiritual and material, and to elevate one's own rules or even habits into universal standards" (p. 13).

To these two principles I would add a third. In perceiving one's own characteristics as universal, a person links himself to humanity. If my "rules and habits" are shared by the race, I am kin to other people on a personal level and can expect acceptance and understanding from them. To carry this argument one step farther, if the characteristics I project onto the race are especially intimate and questionable ones, if they are qualities that have caused me to doubt myself, my acquaintances to furrow their brows, then proving their universality becomes a crucial issue for me. The extent to which I succeed is the extent to which I can affirm myself with dignity. Small wonder that I may spend my lifetime pursuing the goal.

To show how these principles operate in the making of psychology, I will focus on two of the most creative minds the field has known: Sigmund Freud and C. G. Jung. First I will try to draw portraits of Freud and Jung as individuals. Their salient personality traits, their behavior patterns, their aspirations, and their problems will be the objects of my scrutiny. Then I will review their theoretical positions, with particular emphasis on their concepts of human nature, to show how their images of mankind sprang from their experience of themselves and helped them affirm themselves in the most intimate recesses of their being.


## SIGMUND FREUD AND PSYCHOANALYSIS

What kind of a man was Freud? His life has been so thoroughly documented that the question should not be too difficult to answer. Both his own autobiographical writings and the studies done by Jones, Clark, Roazen, Schur, and Sulloway give ample evidence from which to construct a likeness. Appreciations of his character by disciples like Bruno Bettelheim and attacks on his integrity by critics like Jeffrey Masson add qualities to consider. While his admirers emphasize his dedication and brilliance, his detractors his authoritarianism and areas of shortsightedness, for the most part we can let the facts speak for themselves. Whatever interpretations we suggest would, I believe, have been condoned by Freud himself, for they will follow the very principles he taught us.

Sigmund Freud was born on May 6, 1856, in the Moravian town of Freiberg. He grew to manhood in Vienna, the capital city and cultural center of the Austro-Hungarian Empire. This Empire consisted of a conglomeration of diverse states governed (for a reign of 68 years!) by Emperor Francis Joseph, a patriarch whose conservatism led him to eschew the use of electric lighting in his palaces and to delay the construction of a railroad because it would bring in new ideas. Temperamentally opposed to innovation, Francis Joseph was nevertheless determined to turn Vienna into the showplace of Europe, a city to rival Paris in its architectural beauty, industry, science, and art. As a result, the environment in which Freud lived his life—for despite his complaints that he hated the place, he never moved away until he was forced to escape the Nazis a year before his death at eighty-three—became a hub of new ideas, attracting and spawning geniuses in music, literature, and medicine, while providing the breeding ground for movements as diverse as Communism, Zionism, and Naziism. "Gay Vienna," it was popularly called, or sometimes, "the City of Dreams." Ravishing Strauss waltzes, the tantalizing aromas of *Sacher torten* and *Linzer schnitten*, and flirtatious, libertine behavior were in evidence, but these were the indulgences of the favored few. The masses worked a 70-hour week, dined primarily on bread and soup, and grudgingly obeyed the dictates of church and state.

Freud's Vienna, in short, was a center of change, of emerging freethinking, scientific, and hedonistic values, in the midst of a culture still mired in repressive patriarchal morality. Women were considered charming but silly, "sexuality incarnate," yet not supposed to have sexual desires of their own. Children were thought to be innocent but needful of stern control, and the normal person of any age was expected to be both reasonable and obedient, hardworking and thrifty, capable of enjoying life yet chaste (or at least discreet), religious, and patriotic.

Perhaps because of these paradoxes, Vienna was also known for its wry sense of humor. The ironic mode was fully developed among its many writers and journalists, giving rise to such popular slogans as, "Life may be fatal, but not serious," and eventually leading one scion to christen the metropolis *"Kakania"* or *"Kakaland"* (shitland)—from the fact that all official documents were stamped *K.u.K.,* meaning *Koeniglich und Kaiserlich*—Royal and Imperial. That the founder of psychoanalysis should have been reared and educated in such a place is hardly surprising, and part of his outlook on life can be traced to the fact that Freud was a nineteenth century Viennese, not (for instance) a resident of Omaha, Nebraska, or (to bring the analogy closer to the intent of this book) of Zurich, Switzerland.

He was also, of course, the product of a particular family. His father, Jakob, was a merchant engaged primarily in the sale of wool. Married at least once previously[2], Jakob was 20 years older than Sigmund's twenty-one year-old mother, Amalie. He had had two sons by his first wife, one of whom was a year older than Amalie, the other a year younger. By the time of Sigmund's birth, the older son was married and had a child of his own. This boy, Sigmund's nephew John, was to be his closest childhood companion.

When Freud reviewed his childhood as an adult, he declared that his ambivalent feelings toward John had left an indelible mark on his character. "Until the end of my third year we had been inseparable; we had loved each other and fought each other, and, as I have already hinted, this childish relation has determined all my later feelings in my intercourse with persons of my own age. . . . An intimate friend and a hated enemy have always been indispensable to my emotional life; I have always been able to create them anew, and not infrequently my childish ideal has been so closely approached that friend and enemy have coincided in the same person; but not simultaneously, of course, as was the case in my early childhood" (Jones, 1953, pp. 7–8).

While ambivalence toward one's playmates and, in later life, toward one's friends, is not uncommon, Freud's reference to his nephew sheds light on his proclivity to gather followers and expel defectors from the psychoanalytic movement. More than most people, it seems, he craved both intimates and adversaries, a characteristic that contributed to the establishment of his "cause" (according to Jones, the term he always used when referring to psychoanalysis).

In any event, the family was Jewish, but while his parents observed the traditions, Sigmund divested himself of religious belief and became a persuasive proponent of atheism. In "Obsessive Acts and Religious Practices," an essay written in 1907, *Totem and Taboo* (1912), *The Future of an Illusion* (1928), and *Moses and Monotheism* (1939), completed in the year of his death, he puts forth the argument that religious rituals, like obsessive-compulsive acts, are irrational attempts to ward off anxiety or erase guilt feelings whose origins we are afraid to face.

Furthermore, Judeo-Christian religion is based on the model of a father-child relationship in which the child fears his father's wrath but looks to him for protection and love. It is no accident that we pray, "Our Father, who art in Heaven. . . ," for prayer itself is a futile attempt to placate the impersonal forces that control our existence. In reality, these forces are inexorable, but we cast them in the form of a concerned, quasi-human God so we can delude ourselves into believing that we can entreat him to look upon us with favor. In *The Future of an Illusion,* Freud compared religious belief to a mirage that a parched, dying man may "see" in the desert. Considering the sufferer's desperate state, it is understandable that he should envision an oasis amid the burning sands, but his vision is merely the product of wishful fantasy. Freud advises us to find the courage to face our fate without illusion, to place our faith in science and reason, realizing all the while that we are powerless in the face of the inevitable.

This rationalistic, stoical stance was characteristic of the man; but before we examine it more fully, let us look at what was probably the most formative influence on Sigmund's budding temperament—his relationship to his mother. He was her undisputed favorite, a fact that he saw as crucial to his lifelong self-confidence and eventual success. He made frequent reference to this connection, as in *The Interpretation of Dreams* (1900), where he says, "I have found that people who know that they are preferred or favored by their mother give evidence in their lives of a peculiar self-reliance and an unshakable optimism which often seem like heroic attributes and bring actual success to their possessors" (Collected Works, Vol. 5, p. 298).

Amalie Freud was a strong-minded woman. She had eight children in 10 years—a fact that may well have contributed to Freud's fierce competitiveness—but she never wavered in her love for her firstborn son. *"Meine goldener Sigi,"* she called him, and from infancy told him he was destined for greatness.

Slender and pretty in her twenties, imperious in maturity, Amalie has been described in her later years as "a tough old bird." She was "self-willed, fastidious . . . a tyrant to her daughters . . . not easy to live with . . . with great vitality and much impatience . . . a sense of humor that reminds one of Freud's . . . probably the prototype for the regal and self-sufficient type of woman whom Freud was able to admire and understand in his adult life" (Roazen, 1971, p. 45).

There can be little doubt that Sigmund formed an identification with his mother's characteristics. Not only was their sense of humor similar, but he too was exceptionally strong-minded, self-willed, and fastidious. In addition, as he himself confessed, "I do have a tyrannical streak in my nature" (Freud letters, p. 52).

According to Stolorow and Atwood, two psychoanalytic scholars, Freud's relationship to his mother bore all the marks of a "positive Oedipus complex." That is, his knowledge that he was her favorite not only gave him self-confidence, but also led him to idealize their union and divert any hostility he felt toward her onto other objects. "Because of the great emphasis he placed upon it, we may assume that Freud consciously identified most strongly with the simple positive Oedipus complex as he described it in the boy. In this constellation, the source of all conflict lies in the boy's own unruly instinctual desires, and all his aggression is reserved for the father. Through internalization of blame and displacement of hostility the idealized image of the mother is preserved, and the relationship between mother and son remains (as Freud called it) 'altogether the most perfect, the most free from ambivalence of all human relationships' " (Stolorow & Atwood, 1979, p. 64).

With regard to the libidinal aspects of Sigmund's attachment to his mother, Jones says, "Freud had only a few conscious memories of his first three years, as indeed of his first six or seven, but in his self-analysis he . . . recovered a great many of the important ones that had been forgotten . . . One was of penetrating into his parents' bedroom out of (sexual) curiosity and being ordered out by an irate father . . . A more important occurrence . . . was his young brother's death when Sigmund was nineteen months old and the little Julius only eight months. Before the newcomer's birth, the infant Freud had had sole access to his mother's love and milk, and he had to learn from the experience how strong the jealousy of a young child can be. In a letter of 1897, he admits the evil wishes he had against his rival and adds that their fulfillment in his death had aroused self-reproaches, a tendency which had remained ever since. In the same letter, he relates how his libido had been aroused toward his mother, between the ages of two years and two and a half, on the occasion of seeing her naked" (Jones, 1953, pp. 6–7).

Freud's actual words, in the letter to which Jones refers, were ". . . later my libido was stirred up toward *matrem*, namely on the occasion of a journey with her from Leipzig to Vienna, during which we must have spent the night together and I must have had the opportunity of seeing her *nudam*" (Freud letters, p. 262). In an apt exegesis, Christopher Monte (1980) observes, "This passage from Freud's correspondence . . . is remarkable for a number of reasons. First, it is a clear indication of the importance of an idea that Freud had been toying with for some time: namely, that the child experiences sexual impulses toward his mother. . . . The second important aspect of this memory fragment is Freud's admission of such feelings in himself. Notice, however, that both the word for mother *(matrem)* and the word for naked *(nudam)* are in Latin, as though writing them in his native German would have made them all the more unpalatable. Clearly, Freud experienced first hand the kind of emotional resistance that his patients often exhibited" (p. 72).

Freud's relation to his mother, we may conclude, was replete with the qualities he was to claim were characteristic of mother-son relationships in general. Identification and infantile eroticism; possessiveness and jealousy of sibling rivals; death wishes toward those rivals, and guilt if such wishes are satisfied; as well as adult discomfort upon recalling these early emotions; all were parts of Freud's own experience and eventual self-concept. That he came to "discover" these qualities in others was merely an extension of his having discovered them in himself.

Sigmund's father, of course, also served as a role model for his development, but here the boy's feelings were more ambivalent. Reliable, kind, and modest, Jakob won his son's affection, but for all the filial respect Freud bore him, at least one of his father's characteristics was anathema to the boy. A telling incident was recalled with some emotion by the psychoanalyst in his forties. When he was eleven, Jakob had told him of an occasion when he had been walking in the street wearing a new fur cap. "A Christian came up to me," he said, "and with a single blow knocked my cap into the mud and shouted: 'Jew! Get off the pavement!' " Asked how he had responded, Jakob had replied, "I went into the roadway and picked up my cap." Freud still remembered how he had contrasted the situation with the scene in which Hannibal's father had made his son swear to take vengeance on the Romans. As Roazen reports, "Freud was greatly disappointed by his father's response to this . . . insult, and nothing of this passivity . . . remained in Freud when he grew up" (Roazen, 1971, p. 25).

In the summer of 1897, at the age of forty-one, Freud began the self-analysis that was to occupy him for the rest of his life. He recorded and analyzed his dreams, unearthed buried memories from early childhood, followed his own free associations to wherever they might lead, and conscientiously examined his internal dynamics until he had faced himself as nakedly as he expected his patients to do.

That year of 1897 was a watershed in his career, for it was then that he announced his disinterest in further sexual experience and began to devote himself to the building of his psychoanalytic "empire" (another term he frequently used in referring to the movement). It seems significant that the fall of 1896 was the time of his father's death. Shortly after that event, Freud had a dream that led him to admit that he was not as grieved as he should have been. Yet, as he wrote his friend and confidante, Wilhelm Fliess, he had experienced a sense of "being torn up by the roots" and continued to feel this way for months. In *The Interpretation of Dreams* (1900), he averred that a father's death is "the most poignant loss of a man's life" and acknowledged that his own father's passing had played a significant part in motivating his self-analysis.

For our purposes, it is important only to note that Freud's feelings toward his father were as conflicted as he later said everyone's were. Respect and disappointment, love and detachment were mixed in his heart. While he never acknowledged, in his published writings, the parricidal wishes he claimed all sons harbor, we may assume that he would not have denied them to himself.

As Sigmund passed through adolescence, he became more and more concerned about achieving something meaningful in his life. "I seem to remember," he later said, "that through the whole of this time there ran a premonition of a task ahead, till it found open expression in my school-leaving essay as a wish that I might during the course of my life contribute something to our human knowledge" (Clark, 1980, p. 19). While not an unusual ambition in an intelligent young man, the centrality of this desire was remarkable in Freud. Even as a physician, he was more interested in the light his patients' symptoms shed on human nature than in the challenge of curing them of their ills, and the notion that he was destined for fame as a teacher of mankind was never far from his mind. As he also wrote to his friend Fliess, "I have often felt as though I . . . could gladly sacrifice my life for one great moment in history" (Freud letters, p. 203).

Meanwhile, he developed a crush on a girl named Gisela Flüss and, as a revealing aside, became even more enamored of her mother. The lady, both attractive and attentive, took a special interest in the young man, and he in turn placed her on the proverbial pedestal of adoration. According to Clark (1980), "Freud's passion for Frau Flüss was something more than a reaction to kindly mothering; though not sexual passion, it was a feeling within the dictionary definition of 'vehement, commanding, or overpowering emotion' " (p. 25).

Even more revealing, however, is the fact that between this

youthful infatuation and his falling in love with his future wife, Martha Bernays, approximately 10 years were to pass without romantic incident. Despite his later emphasis on sex as the phenomenon of greatest importance in human dynamics, Freud engaged in little sexual activity throughout his life.

Jones (1953) says, "Any physical experiences were probably few and far between," and, "He always gave the impression of being an unusually chaste person—the word 'puritanical' would not be out of place" (p. 172) Freud himself wrote, "I stand for a much freer sexual life. However, I have made little use of such freedom, except insofar as I was convinced of what was permissible for me in this area." His letters to Martha make it clear that in the beginning of their relationship his passion for her was intense, and they did have six children together. Nevertheless, by the age of forty-one he had confided to Fliess, "Sexual excitation is of no more use to a person like me" (Clark, 1980, p. 51). Even by the standards of his time, Freud was decidedly restrained, and when one considers the growing libertinism of the Viennese circles in which he moved, his reserve becomes even more remarkable.

Since the confession to Fliess was made in 1897, the year that marked the beginning of Freud's greatest period of creativity, it seems reasonable to conclude that what the father of psychoanalysis was later to call "sublimation" was now taking place within himself. Freud, it appears, was becoming engaged in a transformation of his own sexual impulses into the investigation of sexual psychodynamics that would last out his lifetime and change the thinking of the western world. In 1896 he had coined the term "psychoanalysis" to designate his psychiatric method. Shortly thereafter, he had disavowed a theory he had publicly proclaimed for several years—the notion that hysteria is based on the seduction or sexual molestation of children by adults, most often of a little girl by her father—replacing it with the theory of infantile sexuality, which suggests that these traumatic "memories" are really the result of the child's incestuous wishes.

Now he was on the verge of creating the entire apparatus of psychoanalytic theory and technique. Many books and essays were to follow—works as technically brilliant as *The Interpretation of Dreams*, as persuasive as *The Psychopathology of Everyday Life*, as speculative as *Moses and Monotheism*, not to mention his outpouring of articles on cases he had treated, matters of psychoanalytic technique, moral questions, cultural questions, and the psychology of artists like Leonardo and Dostoyevski—but by the turn of the century Freud was on his way. He had yet to collaborate and contend with Jung, Adler, Rank, and other gifted contemporaries, he had yet to convince the world to come round to his way of thinking; but from this time on there can be no doubt that Freud had found his calling.

From this time, too, his personal characteristics and thought processes were essentially formed. Before I attempt to describe them, however, let me mention a few more formative influences. First, from the ages of twenty to twenty-six, Freud had worked in the physiological laboratory of the great Ernst Brücke, a man he admired intensely. Brücke's unchallenged authority, no less than his dedication to science and duty, impressed the young student deeply, and he later declared that he had taken him as a role model. Many years previously, Brücke had pledged a solemn oath to support the proposition that there are no other forces within the human organism than those that can be explained by physics and chemistry. This rationalistic, deterministic stance was adopted avidly by Freud, who did not abandon it even when he turned from medical research to analysis of the unconscious.

Second, when he was twenty-nine, Freud had travelled to Paris to study under Jean-Martin Charcot. Charcot was the leading neurologist of the day, a man of erudition and brilliance whom the French called "a prince of science." His reputation was worldwide. Most important to Freud, however, was the fact that Charcot had begun to treat hysterical patients through hypnosis and had demonstrated, time and again, that both their physical and mental symptoms could be relieved by hypnotic suggestion.

Charcot embodied an attitude that was brewing in Freud himself: a rationalistic approach to the irrational, neither denying it nor glorifying it, but attempting to explain it and bring it under the control of reason. That attitude—a fascination with what he was to call the unconscious, combined with an indefatigable effort to discover the laws that govern it—was to remain with Freud throughout his life. Unlike his great contemporaries—Adler, for instance, who had little use for the unconscious, or Jung, who tended to worship it—Freud was driven by a need to explain, in logical terms, the illogicality of the human race. Charcot first showed him a way to do so. No wonder that he wrote to Martha:

> Charcot, who is both one of the greatest physicians and a man whose common sense is of the order of genius, simply demolishes my views and aims. Many a time after a lecture I go out as from Notre Dame . . . My brain is sated as after an evening at the theater. Whether the seed will ever bring forth fruit I do not know; but what I certainly know is that no other human being has ever affected me in such a way. (Jones, 1953, p. 119)

Freud's outlook on life was also influenced by thinkers he admired, such as Darwin and Schopenhauer, and by writers like Goethe and Shakespeare, as well as contemporaries like Melville and Schnitzler. Concepts akin to the wishful unconscious and the sexuality of children were explicit in the writings of his time, for Schopenhauer had proclaimed much earlier that, "the sexual act is the unceasing thought of the unchaste and the ever-recurring daydream of the chaste," while Moll had more recently declared, "The inclination toward the other sex, with all its signs of sexual passion, may be observed long before the onset of puberty."

In Paris, Freud had heard Charcot remark that certain nervous disorders were always a question of "la chose genitale," and back in Vienna his mentor Breuer had observed that neurotic behavior was often related to "the secrets of the marriage bed." His early experience in treating hysterics had convinced him that sexual conflicts were central to this disorder, but other doctors were aware of such possibilities and did not choose to dwell on them. The crucial point, therefore, is that Freud was both ingenious enough and compelled enough to develop these ideas and observations into a special method of treatment, an explanation of psychiatric conditions, and a worldview of vast proportions.

He accomplished these feats through incessant application. Freud's daily routine, for close to 40 years, was to rise at 7, begin seeing patients at 8, break for lunch with his family and a constitutional walk between 1 and 3, continue seeing patients from 3 to 9, have supper, another short walk, and retire to his study to write until 1 or 2 in the morning.

Lest we be left with the impression that he was a thoroughly controlled and therefore placid person, however, it should be mentioned that at least twice, in arguments with Jung, he became so emotionally overwrought that he fainted. He also had bouts of agoraphobia and a recurrent fear of dying. His temperament, it seems, was quite emotional, but his iron self-control was even stronger than his feelings.

According to Clark, Freud was "a self-revealer and a self-concealer," a man who alternately made embarrassing confessions to his friends and then insisted on his privacy, going so far as to burn his letters and notes to keep his personal thoughts concealed from the prying world. Above all, however, he appears to have been a remarkably stoic man. When he was sixty-seven, he developed cancer of the jaw. For 16 years, until his death at eighty-three, he lived with this increasingly painful, debilitating affliction, knowing it would kill him. He endured 33 operations and wore a prosthesis for the last several years of his life.

According to his doctors and closest acquaintances, however, he never bemoaned his fate or gave in to despair or false optimism. Utter realist that he was, he simply observed the progress of the disease, accepted whatever treatment seemed likely to help, and went on with his usual activities—reading, writing, seeing patients and friends, and remaining interested in their concerns until the very end. We tend to think here of his physician Schur's account, according to which Freud determined the timing of the end—"This is agony and makes no sense any more."

"What kind of a man was Freud?" To respond to our initial question, I think it is fair to stress his fortitude, his rationalism, and his self-control. I have used the term "stoical" more than once, for it seems to have been a primary trait. Ambitious he was as well, not for money, but for leaving his mark on the world; recall his adolescent wish "that I might during the course of my life contribute something to our human knowledge." Authoritarian Freud was too, at least in the sense of dominating his "empire" and banishing those who did not agree with him. Hard-working, tenacious, strong-willed, and self-confident: while all these adjectives apply to the man, it is essential to note that his passions were strong, though his defensive system was even stronger. According to Jones (1953), "He was beyond doubt someone whose instincts were far more powerful than those of the average man, but whose repressions were even more potent" (p. 89). Roazen

(1971) agrees: ". . . his emotions, if allowed to be fully generated, were apt to be too much for him, hence the iron control in which he habitually kept himself" (p. 249).

Despite his obsessive interest in the sexual impulses of humanity, Freud was a highly conscientious, morally upright person. He did not "act out," he did not indulge his sexual appetites, he was neither a hedonist nor a profligate. Nor was he meek, mild, and indecisive; nor mystical and starry-eyed. He was a realist, not a romantic, a skeptic, not an idealist. Indeed, it would not be going too far to call him something of a cynic. "In the depths of my heart," he once wrote, "I can't help being convinced that my dear fellow men, with a few exceptions, are worthless" (Freud letters, p. 390). And, "I have found little that is good about human beings on the whole" (Letters of Freud and Pfister, pp. 61–2).

In line with his skepticism, Freud's sense of humor was characteristically Viennese—neither playful nor ribald, but primarily ironic—and characteristically Jewish as well. He did not "kid around," but he often told Jewish jokes to make a point, and in 1938, when the Gestapo forced him to declare that they were a helpful organization before they would allow him to emigrate to England, he wrote, "I can recommend the Gestapo to anyone."

"Psychoanalysis," Freud wrote in his reminiscences, "became the whole of my life." While he remained devoted to his family and cared a good deal about his patients and friends, there can be no doubt that his central goal was the establishment and spread of the movement he had created. Success did not go to his head, but he continued to develop and propound his ideas to the end of his days. The concepts of the unconscious, infantile sexuality, resistance and transference, repression and other defenses, sublimation and all the other categories of psychoanalytic theory were their originator's major concerns. They were the essential substance of his thought.

As far as his personal, internal striving was concerned, however, Freud probably summed it up best in his famous dictum, "Where id was, there shall ego be." Unlike the religions he scorned, which teach us to substitute moral and mystical principles for our basic animal drives, Freud taught the ascendancy of the ego, not the superego, the control of our instincts by reason, not guilt, superstition, or selflessness; and he was his own best pupil.

Having portrayed him in this manner, let us now attempt to decipher Freud's image of humanity. From his theories and treatment techniques, let us see what we can learn about his assumptions and final convictions regarding human nature.

The cornerstone of Freud's theoretical edifice is his concept of the unconscious. The repository of libidinal desire, unacceptable wishes, and unpleasant memories, it constitutes the bulk of the psyche, to which consciousness is as the tip of an iceberg to its base. The implications of this idea are weighty. If we combine Freud's concept of the unconscious with his id-ego-superego triad, we begin to perceive a portrait of the human being as a creature in conflict—partly conscious, but mostly unconscious, partly moral and reasonable, but mostly instinctual—striving to harmonize the opposing forces of impulse and conscience within the boundaries set by reality. Add to that Freud's notion of the mechanisms of defense—repression, regression, rationalization, denial, avoidance, displacement, projection, and the like—and we have an image of a conflicted creature who is also a self-deceiver. While people are capable of insight and honest self-acceptance, for the most part they fail to exercise these capacities, preferring to bolster their opinions of themselves and the figure they wish to cut in the world through a variety of evasive maneuvers.

It is not a sanguine view, but it rises beyond cynicism in allowing for the possibility of growth. Freud thought that even the most mature of persons had areas of neuroticism or unresolved problems stemming from early childhood, but except for the most recalcitrant of cases, improvement was at least conceivable. Those who turned to psychoanalysis or other forms of therapy for help might very well overcome certain conflicts and blind spots, though he insisted that resistance would inevitably play a part in the process. Here again we have a picture of the human being as at odds with himself. He wants to get better, but something within doesn't want to change. Why? Because change for the better, in the Freudian view, involves an honest accounting of oneself, and we all hate to look at the parts of ourselves that we have disguised, prettied up, or blotted out of consciousness.

Another major aspect of Freud's image of humanity is his assumption that sexual wishes play a predominant role in motivating our behavior. Much more than we dare to admit, we are prompted by libidinal drives stemming back to early childhood. Narcissistic, voyeuristic, exhibitionistic, and sadomasochistic impulses are not merely the afflictions of a small number of sexually disturbed individuals, but to greater or lesser extent common to the race. The Oedipus complex is a universal phenomenon. Not only do little boys and girls experience sexual desires directed toward their parents, but adult sexual preferences and problems can often be traced to their origins within the family milieu. All in all, people learn to modify and control their sexuality to conform to the dictates of their society, but under the surface steams a cauldron of lustful desires.

In Freud's personality theory, the goals of human development begin with a progression from "the pleasure principle" to "the reality principle," or from domination by pleasure-seeking drives and the wish for instant gratification to acceptance of the limitations imposed by reality, recognition of other people's rights, and learning to harmonize one's own needs with those of others. Maturity involves fulfillment through "love and work," the two major areas of satisfaction Freud thought were valid. "Genitality," a term he used for the attainment of psychosexual maturity, implies the outgrowing of predominantly "oral," "anal," and "phallic" forms of gratification, though the fact is that most adults retain characteristics based on these forms. It is all-important to sublimate one's infantile drives into socially useful activities, and one must increase one's consciousness considerably by uncovering one's repressions, examining childhood memories, and learning to understand one's unconscious. The Freudian techniques of free association, dream interpretation, analysis of slips of the tongue, purposeful forgetting, symbolic acts, and transference reactions to one's analyst are means to these ends.

Psychoanalysis is a long, hard process requiring perseverance and tenacity in the face of one's resistances. Its primary goal is self-knowledge or insight accompanied by abreaction or cathartic release of buried emotions. It is not, however, an invitation to displays of unrestrained emotionality, to the gut-level expression of feelings and "letting it all hang out" recommendations of certain post-Freudian groups. Nor is it a promoter of licentious behavior, of irresponsible or casual sex. Neither is it in any sense an attempt to attain a spiritual orientation, a religious or mystical outlook on life. Freud holds out no promises of radical rebirth, instant happiness, or everlasting peace of mind. With effort and courage, he suggests, one may "transform neurotic misery into common unhappiness"—an extremely sober opinion of what we can hope to attain in attempting to overcome our problems.

As you know, it is my contention that the vision underlying these conceptions of the workings, problems, and developmental possibilities of human nature grew out of the workings, problems, and development of Sigmund Freud himself. I am tempted to say that the correspondences should be obvious by now, but since they may seem obvious only to me, let me attempt to spell them out.

As a nineteenth century Viennese man, a Jewish doctor of the upper middle class, educated and literate, Freud was heir to a number of common outlooks. Both skepticism and irony were parts of the liberal Jewish tradition with which he allied himself, as they were of the sophisticated Viennese in general. One could hardly be a freethinking Viennese Jew of his time and not believe that people were basically dissemblers and prevaricators. To hold this view in a general way, however, is not uniquely Freudian; asserting that the secrets we harbor are primarily sexual in nature, that they hark back to early childhood, and include such motives as the child's sexual feelings toward its parents, its competitiveness and even death wishes toward rivals within the family, begins to define the Freudian position. To expand the sexual theory (and attendant notions of how we are ruled by childish needs and unconscious conflicts) into an explanation of phenomena as diverse as dreams, art, and religion, is to march with Freud as he steadily broadened the scope of his ideas. That he carried them too far, however, almost all his detractors agree.[3] Their unanimous objection is that he was so enamored of his sexual theory that he could not put it in proper perspective.

How does this relate to the man? Freud, you may recall, undertook his self-analysis in 1897. He and Breuer had published *Studies in Hysteria* in 1895, so we know that by then he had formed the idea that sexual factors lay behind neurotic symptoms. Indeed, in a letter written in 1894, he had confessed to Fliess, "They regard me rather as a monomaniac, while I have the distinct feeling that I have touched on one of the great secrets of nature (i.e. the importance of sexuality in neuroses)" (*Origins of the Psychoanalytic Movement*, p. 83).

The concept of the Oedipus complex was developed a few years later, for it was in 1897 that Freud forsook his seduction theory in favor of the concept of childhood sexuality, and the full-fledged theory of the Oedipus complex first appeared in *The Interpretation of Dreams,* written in 1899 and published in 1900. It was also in 1897 that Freud wrote Fliess that he had lost interest in personal sexual excitation, and from then on (though it obviously began a little earlier) he appeared to dwell so predominantly on sexuality that he alienated many colleagues.

That a Viennese doctor, resident of a city whose cultural elite were indulging in libertine living, should have reawakened the world to the ubiquitousness of sex is probably not mere coincidence. "Gay Vienna's" relation to the repressive morality of the Austro-Hungarian Empire was analogous to Freud's relation to the bourgeois world. His discovery of the Oedipus complex, however, was entirely original. Stolorow and Atwood, the psychologists quoted earlier, pointed out that Sigmund himself had been a clear-cut case of a boy with a "positive Oedipus complex." His youthful adoration of his mother was noteworthy, his identification with her exceptional. It was his mother who firmly believed that *"goldene Sigi"* would become a great man. As further evidence of the part she played in his emotional development, Freud's primary love-object during adolescence was a mother-figure—Frau Flüss—and his wife's role in their relationship had obvious maternal overtones. Martha not only cooked and kept house for him (almost all wives did that), but laid out his clothes each morning and applied the toothpaste to his toothbrush to help him prepare for the day. That the Oedipus complex theory was a stroke of genius cannot be denied; nor should it be denied that its roots were embedded in its creator's personal experience.

Freud's overemphasis on sex was a direct result of the fact that he sublimated his personal urges into a preoccupation with the phenomenon in the world at large. This conclusion is supported, undeniably, it seems to me, by the fact that the years in which he lost interest in personal sexual satisfaction were the very years in which he solidified his theoretical position.

The kind of sexual freedom fostered by Freudian psychology, furthermore, was more in line with Freud's own temperament than with the changes that were taking place in the world. "Look, don't touch," could have been its motto, for psychoanalysis, in the image of its founder, encouraged the examination of all sexual impulses, while frowning on licentious behavior. As Freud could not condone the acting out of his own urges, the therapy he devised looked askance at promiscuity in its patients.

Over and above his sexual interests, however, Freud was dedicated to a rational explanation of the irrational. The fundamental task he had chosen in life was *to make sense* of the dreams and fantasies, self-defeating behavior, neurotic symptoms, and delusions that afflict the human race. His abiding reputation is a testament to his success. The system of treatment he designed, however, is committed to having its patients do the same. What Sigmund Freud recommended for the salvation of others was precisely what had most meaning for Sigmund Freud.

I do not intend to suggest that he should (or could) have done otherwise. It is perfectly understandable that, in offering the world the best of which he was capable, he prescribed the remedy that had worked most effectively for him. For others like him, it frequently works well, too. The problem is that not everyone has proved to be similar to the founder of psychoanalysis, which is why many people cannot benefit from psychoanalysis and have to turn to other forms of therapy for help.

In the last analysis, Freud's method of treatment, like his theory of personality, is modelled ingeniously on his own psychodynamics. Subject your unconscious to rational scrutiny, he advises us; root out your infantile drives; unearth your buried memories; decipher your dreams; acknowledge your defensiveness; give up your magical thinking; and learn to control your impulses. The silent addendum is: these efforts helped me come to terms with myself, so they should help you, too. Unfortunately, both his treatment and his theories have limited applicability to the rest of the human race. Not everyone can do what Freud advises, and when they try, not everyone feels better as a result.

This would pose no problem if Freud had not maintained that his ideas were universally true and that only "resistance" held others back from acknowledging them. His arrogation of absolute truth is the major blot on the great man's record as a teacher of humanity. What compelled him to make the claim? A Freudian answer might be that this beloved son of an ambitious mother could not relinquish his infantile omnipotence, which would also help explain why he considered the psychoanalytic movement his "empire." The "tyrannical streak" he himself acknowledged was so central a characteristic, perhaps, that it was never outgrown.

Such an answer would have the virtue of indicating that great achievements can arise out of infantile traits, a principle that dips into the pool of paradox at the heart of the human condition. I think we do Freud as much justice, however, if we suggest that his need to maintain the ultimate truth of his theories was based on the fact that his very identity was bound up with them. By projecting his own psychodynamics onto the psychodynamics of the race, he had universalized himself, thereby giving his life its greatest significance. To admit the possibility that his ideas had only relative validity would have been too deflating, for he was totally immersed in them. To understand Freud in his fullness, we must take to heart the remark from his reminiscences, "Psychoanalysis became the whole of my life."

## C. G. Jung and Analytical Psychology

Carl Gustav Jung was a remarkably different kind of person. In *his* reminiscences, he wrote:

> When people say I am wise, or a sage, I cannot accept it. . . . The difference between most people and myself is that for me the "dividing walls" are transparent. . . . For me the world has from the beginning been infinite and ungraspable . . . [and speaking of his creativity:] There was a daimon in me, and in the end its presence proved decisive. It overpowered me, and if I was at times ruthless it was because I was in the grip of the daimon . . . I had to obey an inner law which was imposed on me and left me no freedom of choice. (*Memories, Dreams, Reflections*, pp. 355–57)

Not nearly as cryptic as much of Jung's writing, these statements may begin to give us a sense of the man. Our impression should include his own sense of destiny, his belief that he (and others) are put on this earth for a purpose, that human life is not random but has inherent meaning, though that meaning is too profound for us fully to grasp. It should also take note of his remark about the transparency of his "dividing walls," for Jung was so radically open to the unconscious that it made him seem, to some, a genius whose vision extended beyond time and place, while to others he was, at times at least, as close to psychotic as many great geniuses are.

If Jung's contribution to personality theory could be summed up in one grand conclusion (which of course it cannot), that conclusion might make reference to the title of one of his books. *Modern Man in Search of a Soul* (a collection of essays for a popular audience, published in 1933) touches on the essence of Jung's point of view. We have lost contact with our spirituality, he tells us, and that is the core of our problems. Conventional religion has failed us; it no longer provides a convincing vehicle for the enlightened person; and in contradiction to Freud, science and reason are no substitute. Immersing oneself in the unconscious, however, as Jung himself felt compelled to do, may reconnect us to our souls.

His focus on spirituality suggests that Jung was as much a metaphysician as a psychiatrist or psychologist and, indeed, his preoccupation with the occult was one of the major factors that came between him and Freud. The humility contained in such statements as, "When people say I am wise, or a sage, I cannot accept it," was part of his stance. So too, however, was the opposite. Near the end of his life, when a reporter from the BBC asked him if he believed in God, he calmly replied, "I don't need to believe. I know" (*Face to Face*, interview conducted by John Freeman in 1959). This attitude led Freud to call him "sanctimonious," and others to accuse him of thinking that "he had a hot line to God" (Anthony Storr, quoted in Brome, 1981, p. 232).

Talk about paradox! Jung was nothing if not an embodiment of "the coincidence of opposites," one of the central themes of his theorizing. If his conception of the psyche could be portrayed in a visual symbol, it would undoubtedly be the yang-yin image of Oriental philosophy:

Darkness and light, male and female, spirit and earth, good and evil, emotion and reason, intuition and sensation: all are intertwined in the totality of our being.

That this image was of great significance to him is not surprising when we learn from one of his biographers that Jung was a "chameleon personality . . . rich in contradictions . . . the man firmly anchored in reality who enjoyed good food, sailing, pipe-smoking and mountaineering, and the metaphysician who was fascinated by the occult. He could move with disconcerting speed from the loftiest speculation to an analysis of good coffee-making, cook an excellent meal, swear eloquently, and face a threatening mob . . . with immense courage . . . Jung was a man capable of great rages, sometimes the result of a long accumulation of repressed aggression, but he rarely held a grudge. . . . He could literally eject a visitor who had become intolerable, and his invective against his enemies included phrases like 'slimy bastard,' 'empty gasbag,' 'a pisspot of unconscious devils,' and might even mount to the point of physical threats. . . . In total contradiction, he was the sensitive scholar who carried intelligence into the high places of intellect . . . (and) half his life was spent speculating about the nature of Man" (Brome, 1981, pp. 18–20).

Carl Gustav Jung was born on July 26, 1875, in the village of Kesswil, near Basel. He grew up in Basel and in his twenties moved to Zurich, where he lived for the rest of his life. Switzerland during Jung's formative years was a country of firm moral standards. The sanctity of the family was unquestioned, sexual freedom was taboo, the church was a potent force, and the Protestant ethic dominated most people's aspirations. That it was also a more problematical society than its public image suggests is attested to by various Swiss scholars.

According to Herbert Kubly, the Swiss "would like to be friendly but don't know how" (*Native's Return*, 1981). They are too insular, too suspicious, too stiff and formal. Their public posture is polite and punctual, efficient, honest, and practical, but behind this facade lies a great deal of internal tension. In Jung's time, there was virtually no acceptance of sex as fun, of the game of love as one of life's sweet delights. Zurich at night had a thriving commerce in prostitution, but all day long the bells of dozens of churches reminded the citizens of their allegiance.

According to Jolande Jacobi, one of Jung's closest disciples, "The legendary Swiss efficiency is real enough when they deal with inanimate materials, with controllable objects like chemicals, fine instruments, machines. But their efficiency falls apart completely when it is confronted with people. . . . Jealousy and fear are dominant emotions, they are afraid of opening their homes to you, afraid that you may learn the secrets of their domestic life. One of the greatest Swiss fears is sex. . . . There is an absolute lack of communication on a physical level. There is none of the sensitivity of the French, the lust of the Italian, or even the sentimentality of the German. Attitudes about sex are completely unnatural. It's either sacred or profane—the wife or the whore—and both are unnatural" (quoted in Kubly, 1981, pp. 121–124). Jacobi may have exaggerated, but when I lived in Zurich in the 1950s I was told a joke at the C. G. Jung Institute that seemed to confirm her view. According to this story, "There are only two kinds of Swiss women—virgins and matrons. In between, they visit England."

Finally, according to Jung, "For a Swiss a new idea is something like an unknown dangerous animal which is to be avoided . . . or at least approached with caution" (quoted in Kubly, 1981). Every nation, of course, fosters a complex of attitudes and behavior patterns that cannot be summed up in simple slogans. The Swiss, in Jung's time as today, must have included many kinds of personalities, many levels of sophistication, many outlooks and traditions. Nevertheless, each nation in a given era does have dominant characteristics that distinguish it from others, and the point I want to make is that growing up in Basel must have been a significantly different experience than growing up in Vienna. On that basis alone, Jung and Freud were bound to have different viewpoints, at least in regard to sex.

As irony, however, rules all human affairs, Freud preached the importance of sex but was himself more chaste than most men of his time, while Jung preached the greater importance of spirituality but, as we shall see, indulged his sexual impulses while the church bells of Zurich rang on.

To return to his childhood, Carl was raised in a home with a distinctly religious atmosphere. His father was one of a long line of pastors, though he was not sustained by his faith. Depressed and unhappy in his marriage, he was good to his children (Carl had one sister, 9 years younger) but unable to provide them with financial security or an inspiring role model. As a result, he struck his son as a somewhat pathetic figure.

Jung described his mother, in contrast, as "a dual personality." Outwardly a hearty maternal figure, she privately gave vent to mutterings at odds with her public attitudes and "emanated influences" that frightened and fascinated her offspring. Her father was said to have had visions and conversed with the world of the spirits, and at night, Jung recalled, she was "equally mysterious."

When Carl was three, his mother spent several months in a Basel hospital, apparently because of a mental disorder. "From then on," he later declared, "I have always felt mistrustful when the word 'love' was spoken. The feeling I associated with 'woman' was for a long time that of innate unreliability. 'Father,' on the other hand, meant reliability and—powerlessness" (*Memories, Dreams, Reflections*, 1961, p. 8).

Age three to four, according to Jung, was a decisive period in his development. "At that time," he wrote, "I . . . had vague fears at night. I would hear things walking about in the house. The muted roar of the Rhine Falls was always audible and all around lay a danger zone. People drowned, bodies were swept over the rocks. In the cemetery nearby, the sexton would dig a hole—heaps of brown, upturned earth. Black, solemn men in long frock coats with unusually tall hats and shiny black boots would bring a black box. My father would be there in his clerical gown, speaking in a resounding voice. Women wept. I was told that someone was being buried in this hole in the ground . . ." Around that time, he had the earliest dream he could remember, a dream which he said "was to preoccupy me all my life."

The vicarage stood quite alone near Laufen castle, and there was a big meadow stretching back from the sexton's farm. In the dream I was in this meadow. Suddenly I discovered a dark, rectangular, stone-lined hole in the ground. I had never seen it before. I ran forward curiously and peered down into it. Then I saw a stone stairway leading down. Hesitantly and fearfully, I descended. At the bottom was a doorway with a round arch, closed off by a green curtain. It was a big heavy curtain of worked stuff like brocade, and it looked very sumptuous. Curious to see what might be hidden behind, I pushed it aside. I saw before me in the dim light a rectangular chamber about thirty feet long. The ceiling was arched and of hewn stone. The floor was laid with flagstones, and in the center a red carpet ran from the entrance to a low platform. On this platform stood a wonderfully rich golden throne. I am not certain, but perhaps a red cushion lay on the seat. It was a magnificent throne, a real king's throne in a fairy tale. Something was standing on it which I thought at first was a tree trunk twelve to fifteen feet high and about one and a half to two feet thick. It was a huge thing, reaching almost to the ceiling. But it was of a curious composition: it was made of skin and naked flesh, and on top there was something like a rounded head with no face and no hair. On the very top was a single eye, gazing motionlessly upward.

It was fairly light in the room, although there were no windows and no apparent source of light. Above the head, however, was an aura of brightness. The thing did not move, yet I had the feeling that it might at any moment crawl off the throne like a worm and creep toward me. I was paralyzed with terror. At that moment I heard from outside and above me my mother's voice. She called out, "Yes, just look at him. That is the man-eater!" That intensified my terror still more, and I awoke sweating and scared to death. (*Memories, Dreams, Reflections*, 1961, pp. 13–15)

When he recalled this dream as an adult, Jung ascribed to it a prospective meaning. The phallic creature on the throne he saw as an underworld deity related to the phallic worship of certain non-Christian religions; the fact that his mother called it "the man-eater" he associated with a prayer[4] she had taught him, from which he had gotten the notion that Jesus devoured little children to protect them from Satan; the hole in the ground he related to his observation of the burial ceremonies at which his father presided. In sum, it referred to death and the hereafter, to non-Christian religion and the dark side of God—all themes that would preoccupy him as a scholar and investigator of the unconscious. Summing up his interpretation, he wrote,

Through this childhood dream I was initiated into the secrets of the earth. What happened then was a kind of burial in the earth, and many years were to pass before I came out again. Today I know that it happened in order to bring the greatest possible amount of light into the darkness. My intellectual life had its unconscious beginnings at that time. (*Memories, Dreams, Reflections*, 1961, p. 15)

Whether we agree with this explanation or prefer a more

Freudian view of the sexual concerns and death anxieties of this precocious child, it is certainly remarkable that he would have had such a dream at all, remembered it, and found significance in it for his entire life. But that was Jung's *modus operandi*. In his autobiography, for instance, he makes much more frequent reference to his dreams and visions than to relationships with family, friends, and colleagues, the establishment of the C. G. Jung Institute, or other significant actions. "In the end," he declares, "the only events in my life worth telling are those when the imperishable world irrupted into this transitory one." Not everyone would concur—indeed, some have said that precisely in this manner did Jung avoid responsibility for his more dubious acts—but the point is that he defined himself primarily as a vehicle of the eternal, a protagonist in God's evolving plan for the human race.

As a child, Carl often played alone. A highly imaginative youngster, his fantasies occasionally became so vivid that they could have been called hallucinations. For example, recorded in *Memories, Dreams, Reflections*, 1961:

> At night mother was strange and mysterious. One night I saw coming from her door a faintly luminous, indefinite figure whose head detached itself from the neck and floated along in front of it, in the air, like a little moon. (p. 81)

> About my seventh year . . . I was sick with pseudo-croup, accompanied by choking fits. One night during an attack I stood at the foot of the bed, my head bent back over the bed rail, while my father held me under the arms. Above me I saw a glowing blue icicle about the size of the full moon, and inside it moved golden figures which I thought were angels. This vision was repeated, and each time it allayed my fear of suffocation. (pp. 18–19).

It seems significant that his visionary experiences had a healing as well as a disturbing effect, for as an analyst Jung would be the first to emphasize the healing power of the unconscious.

During his preadolescent years, Carl engaged in a secret ritual which was full of portent for his later development. He had a favorite stone in his garden and, as he says,

> "Often, when I was alone, I sat down on this stone, and then

began an imaginary game that went something like this: 'I am sitting on top of this stone and it is underneath.' But the stone also could say 'I' and think: 'I am lying here on this slope and he is sitting on top of me.' The question then arose: 'Am I the one who is sitting on the slope or am I the stone on which he is sitting?' This question always perplexed me, and I would stand up, wondering who was what now. . . . My disunion with myself and uncertainty in the world at large led me to an action which at the time was quite incomprehensible to me. I had in those days (10 years of age) a yellow, varnished pencil case of the kind commonly used by primary-school pupils, with a little lock and the customary ruler. At the end of this ruler I now carved a little manikin, about two inches long, with frock coat, top hat, and shiny black boots. I colored him black with ink, sawed him off the ruler, and put him in the pencil case, where I made him a little bed. I even made a coat for him out of a bit of wool. In the case I also placed a smooth, oblong blackish stone from the Rhine, which I had painted with water colors to look as though it were divided into an upper and lower half, and had long carried around in my trouser pocket. This was *his* stone. All this was a great secret. Secretly I took the case to the forbidden attic at the top of the house . . . and hid it with great satisfaction on one of the beams under the roof—for no one must ever see it! I knew that not a soul would ever find it there. No one could discover my secret and destroy it. I felt safe, and the tormenting sense of being at odds with myself was gone . . . (p. 20)

This possession of a secret had a very powerful formative influence on my character; I consider it the essential factor of my boyhood. . . . The manikin was a little cloaked god of the ancient world, a Telesphoros such as stands on the monuments of Asklepios and reads to him from a scroll . . . When I was in England in 1920, I carved out of wood two similar figures without having the slightest recollection of that childhood experience. One of them I had reproduced on a large scale in stone, and this figure now stands in my garden in Kusnacht. Only when I was doing this work did the unconscious supply me with a name. It called the figure Atmavictu—the "breath of life." It was a further development of that fearful tree of my childhood dream, which was now revealed as the "breath of life," the creative impulse." (p. 33)

Meanwhile, however, he also developed a strong distaste for the church and its preachings. Aware of his father's religious disillusionment, Carl felt that the rituals through which he had led him, including his first communion, were hollow and hypocritical. Yet the boy's internal sense of a link to God, whom he had already begun to conceive of as a far more awesome force than the civilized Christian Deity, only waxed as his piety waned. Finally, when he was twelve or thirteen, he experienced a revelation that he later said "overshadowed my whole life."

> One fine summer day . . . I came out of school at noon and went to the cathedral square. The sky was gloriously blue, the day one of radiant sunshine. The roof of the cathedral glittered, the sun sparkling from the new, brightly glazed tiles. I was overwhelmed by the beauty of the sight, and thought: "The world is beautiful and the church is beautiful, and God made all this and sits above it far away in the blue sky on a golden throne and . . ." Here came a great hole in my thoughts, and a choking sensation. I felt numbed, and knew only: "Don't go on thinking now! Something terrible is coming, something I don't want to think . . .

(After 3 restless nights and days in which he decided that "God in His omniscience had arranged everything so that the first parents would have to sin, therefore it was God's intention that they should sin," and concluded that God was arranging a decisive test for him),

> I gathered all my courage, as though I were about to leap forthwith into hell-fire, and let the thought come. I saw before me the cathedral, the blue sky. God sits on His golden throne, high above the world—and from under the throne an enormous turd falls upon the sparkling new roof, shatters it, and breaks the walls of the cathedral asunder.

> So that was it! I felt an enormous, an indescribable relief. Instead of the expected damnation, grace had come upon me, and with it an unutterable bliss such as I had never known. . . . After that experience I knew what God's grace was. One must be utterly abandoned to God; nothing matters but fulfilling His will . . . Why did God befoul His cathedral? That, for me, was a terrible thought. But then came the dim understanding that God could be something terrible." (pp. 36–40)

These youthful memories convey an impression of the kind

of man Jung was to become. As imaginative and in touch with the occult as his mother (indeed, he was to call himself, as he had called her, "a dual personality"), as preoccupied with religious issues as his father (though, in contrast to his father's disillusioned piety, he was convinced of a personal connection to a most unconventional God), he was also an original. Reinforcing Brome's description of him as "a chameleon personality . . . rich in contradictions," Jacobi recalled that "contemplativeness and childlike cheerfulness, delicate sensibility and robust simplicity, cold reserve and true devotion, rigor and tolerance, humor and severity, aloofness and love for mankind were equally prominent traits in his makeup" (quoted in *The Swiss,* by Walter Sorell, 1972). Above all, we must see, he had a rich inner life that provided him with refuge and relief from stress, as well as a growing conviction that salvation could come from submitting to the unconscious.

As a student at the University of Basel, Jung became interested in a fifteen-year-old cousin who was achieving recognition as a medium. She held seances in which she supposedly contacted the dead, predicted the future, spoke in strange tongues, and evoked other eerie phenomena. Jung attended her seances for two years, assembling observations that eventually became a part of his doctoral dissertation, *On the Psychology and Pathology of So-Called Occult Phenomena* (his first major work, published in 1902).

Although she was finally caught red-handed in an act of outright deception, his cousin's performance, Jung concluded, was a mixture of fraudulence, multiple personality, and genuine psychic ability. In a deeply thought-out analysis of the interlocking relationship between psychological and spiritual phenomena, he adopted a stance that he would maintain throughout his life. Spiritual forces, he insisted, are real; they evade our understanding because they neither obey the law of cause and effect nor function within the confines of our space-time continuum. People in altered states of consciousness are most susceptible to these forces, although it is sometimes true that reports of psychic experiences are the result of delusional thinking.

That this stance was consonant with his mother's "dual personality," as well as his own, should be clear. By forming the view that contact with the "other world" could either be a sign of pathology or a gift to be cherished and cultivated, Jung allowed himself the freedom to examine his own mind as a psychiatrist while attempting to validate his unusual sensibilities and follow them into unexplored depths of being. In any case, he began to devote a great deal of energy to studying esoteric texts. Obscure philosophical treatises, Oriental scrolls, archaeological documents, medieval manuscripts, and Gnostic writings absorbed his interest. In time he would write an entire volume on alchemy as a precursor not to modern chemistry but to Jungian psychology, and eventually he would conceive of an acausal principle—synchronicity— to explain such mysteries as meaningful coincidences and dreams that foretell the future.

Meanwhile, however, as a medical student, Jung was bright but erratic, capable of getting drunk and behaving abrasively, but consumed with ambition for future success. While studying for final exams, he opened Krafft-Ebing's *Lehrbuch der Psychiatre*, and as he recalled, "My heart . . . began to pound. I had to stand up and draw a deep breath. My excitement was intense for it had become clear . . . that for me the only possible goal was psychiatry" (Brome, 1981, p. 70). What made this decision so compelling? In his BBC interview, Jung said that psychiatry afforded him an opportunity to unite his interests in natural science and philosophy. His excitement, however, must have had much more personal significance. I think it is not unreasonable to suggest that psychiatry held out the possibility of explaining his own aberrant mental experiences.

In 1903, Carl married Emma Rauschenbach, the daughter of a wealthy industrialist. She was twenty-one, a girl of good education and upright moral character; he was twenty-eight and on his way to establishing himself as a psychiatrist. Four daughters and a son were born to them between 1904 and 1914, and they were to live together for the rest of their lives; but by 1913 Jung had become involved with a younger woman, Antonia (Toni) Wolff, and despite his wife's dismay, he insisted on maintaining an intimate relationship with her for several decades.

Toni had been a patient of Jung's when he first became her lover, and it has recently come to light that he had sexual affairs with other patients as well.[5] In his time, as today, such relationships were considered unethical. In Puritan Zurich, they must have been judged as scandalous. Small wonder, then, that Jung had no wish to make them public. More remarkable, however, is the fact that his double life with Emma and Toni was no secret within the Jungian circle and that he went so far as to insist, at one point, that the women receive counseling to help them accept each other.

Soon after their marriage, Carl and Emma built a beautiful home in Kusnacht, a suburb of Zurich, where they continued to live with their children. . In his forties, however, Jung constructed a retreat for himself on a piece of land he had bought about 20 miles away. Called "The Tower," it was a stone structure built on a circular plan, with a central hearth for cooking, but no electricity or running water. When he was there, no one was allowed to visit without his permission. Dividing his time between these two abodes, as he did his affection between Toni and Emma, seems as much a manifestation of his duality as any of the other contradictions in his character.

When Jung met Freud in 1907, he had published *Studies in Word Association* and *The Psychology of Dementia Praecox,* but he had not yet enunciated principles that could be called a theory of personality. When he broke with Freud in 1913, his theoretical position was beginning to take shape, and by 1921, when he published *Psychological Types,* it can be said to have been formed.

In the latter work, he formulated the concept of *introversion-extroversion* and what he called *"the four functions"*—thinking, feeling, sensation, and intuition. According to his theory, these are the personality dimensions along which all of us can be located. We each tend to display a certain amount of introversion and extroversion; we each have greater or lesser access to our capacities for logical thought, emotional reactions, sensory awareness, and intuitive grasp of implicit meanings. Above all, however, the principles of balance, complementariness, or *enantiodromia* rule our psyches. The person, for example, who is primarily extroverted in overt behavior, will have an equal amount of introverted potential living an underground existence; one who relies on thinking and intuition to cope with life's problems, must harbor unconscious potentials of feeling and sensation waiting for release. A fully developed or "individuated" man or woman, Jung implied, would have open access to all four functions as well as being capable of both introverted and extroverted orientations.

The image that informs this view is so clearly modelled on Jung's own character that it seems amazing that no commentator on his theories has seen fit to discuss the correspondence. That a man in whom duality of motives was a primary trait—who was himself both introverted and extroverted to remarkable degrees; who was himself first torn and then made whole by the opposition and integration of his thinking and feeling, sensation and intuitive functions—should have declared that these were the basic constructs of human nature can hardly be fortuitous. That there was substantial truth in Jung's insight into personality dynamics is attested by his worldwide reputation, but that his own personality served as springboard to his theory cannot be denied. Furthermore, in suggesting that individuation demands recognition and acceptance of all one's conflicting drives, this man "rich in contradictions," this "sensitive scholar" who was capable of "great rages," this individual of "delicate sensibility and robust simplicity, cold reserve and true devotion" was prescribing his own mode of resolution to the rest of the world.

It is, we may feel, an inspiring mode, and the vision behind it—the vision of wholeness or what is today called "owning" all our faculties and inclinations—is shared by psychologists of many persuasions. Nevertheless, C. G. Jung was compelled to present it as persuasively as he could so that he could affirm himself in the process of enlightening his readers.

As central to Jungian theory as the concepts of introversion-extroversion and the four functions, however, is the concept of the *collective unconscious*. This idea, with its attendant notion of the *archetypes* that characterize and rule the depths of our psyches, was formulated in the years just preceding and following the breakup with Freud.[6] Persona, Shadow, Anima/animus, Hero, Child, Wise Old Man, Earth Mother, and Self: these and other figures of mythological proportions, said Jung, inhabit the unconscious realms of all human beings, personifying universal tendencies, needs, and capacities to which every person is subject. The collective unconscious and its archetypes are universal and eternal; they link us to the entire history of the race and are inherent to our existence. Coming to terms with oneself involves coming to terms with them.

As is by now widely known, the Persona represents the facades or masks we present to the outer world, the various ways in which we attempt to be charming, impressive, or at least acceptable to others. The Shadow, in contrast, represents those qualities we try to hide. Our lust, our hostility, our greed, our vanity, our pettiness, our miserliness, our callousness, or whatever characteristics we are ashamed to acknowledge adhere to our Shadow, while our intelligence, kindness, courage, loyalty, or whatever else we are proud to display adhere to our Persona.

Once again, it is clear, we are faced with a pair of opposites in Jungian theory, and once again, it is equally clear, they are absolutely typical of the theorist himself. According to those who knew him best, Jung was as brilliant, charming, and impressive as a man could well be; according to those who knew him but had reason to be critical of him, he was also ruthless and overbearing, sanctimonious and inconsiderate. In fact, he probably possessed all these characteristics to a greater degree than the average person, which is why the images of Persona and Shadow loomed so large on his mental horizon.

Jung himself wrote eloquently about his encounters with the Anima, Hero, Child, and other archetypal figures in his autobiography. His entire system of thought, however, culminates in the concept of the Self; so it is important for us to see how this force relates to the man's own dynamics. The Self is Jung's term for what Emerson called "the Oversoul," the essentially incomprehensible divinity that determines our destinies, the most profound, all-encompassing spiritual force that comprises our core. Few people, he believed, either achieve or can stand a direct confrontation with the Self—much as the ancients believed that it would be overwhelming to look upon the face of God. Jung's Self, however, is different than the Judeo-Christian image of God in that the Self is beyond morality as we conceive it, beyond good and evil, beyond cause and effect. It is a force whose overriding purpose appears to be to increase consciousness, bring light into darkness, not to ensure the petty happiness or success of ordinary mortals.[7]

Recall Jung's statement about his earliest childhood dream—"Today I know that it happened in order to bring the greatest possible amount of light into the darkness"—and his response to the BBC interviewer's question as to whether he believed in God—

"I don't need to believe. I know." Other references to his encounters with the Self abound in his writings, so there can be no
doubt that he conceived of himself as a man of destiny, one whose
fate it was to make manifest the will of the guiding force of the
universe. Perhaps it was this, above all, that led some disciples
to see him as an inspired prophet,[8] while provoking critics to sneer
at his presumptuousness.

In his autobiography, Jung related a dream that he said led
him to the concept of the collective unconscious.

> I was in a house I did not know, which had two stories. It was
> "my house." I found myself in the upper story, where there was
> a kind of salon . . . I wondered that this should be my house, and
> thought, "Not bad." But then it occurred to me that I did not know
> what the lower floor looked like. Descending the stairs, I reached
> the ground floor. There everything was much older, and I realized
> that this part of the house must date from about the fifteenth or
> sixteenth century. The furnishings were medieval; the floors were
> of red brick. Everywhere it was rather dark. I went from one room
> to another, thinking, "Now I must explore the whole house." I
> came upon a heavy door and opened it. Beyond it I discovered a
> stone stairway that led down into the cellar. Descending again, I
> found myself in a beautifully vaulted room which looked exceed-
> ingly ancient. Examining the walls, I discovered layers of brick
> among the ordinary stone blocks, and chips of brick in the mortar.
> As soon as I saw this I knew that the walls dated from Roman
> times. My interest was now intense. I looked more closely at the
> floor. It was of stone slabs, and in one of these I discovered a ring.
> When I pulled it, the stone slab lifted and again I saw a stairway
> of narrow stone steps leading down into the depths. These, too, I
> descended and entered a low cave cut into the rock. Thick dust
> lay on the floor, and in the dust were scattered bones and broken
> pottery, like the remains of a primitive culture. I discovered two
> human skulls, obviously very old and half disintegrated. Then I
> awoke. (*Memories, Dreams, Reflections*, 1961, pp. 158–159).

In his BBC interview, on the other hand, he said it was his
discovery that the thinking of a psychotic patient corresponded
to an ancient Mithraic text—both focused on "the phallus of the
sun" which "swings to and fro causing the winds to blow"—that
led him to the discovery of the collective unconscious. The dis-

crepancy was characteristic of the man. Both inner and outer experiences enhanced his sense of primordial truth, but distinguishing between them was not important. He might, in fact, have thought it misleading.

Since I had the opportunity to speak to Jung when he was in his eighties, I would like to add my impression of him at that time to the portrait I have been sketching. Let me first explain how I came to see him. In 1955–1956, I was awarded a postdoctoral fellowship to attend the C. G. Jung Institute. While in training there, I developed serious reservations about my allegiance to the Jungian group. Some of the teachers, I felt, promoted a cultlike atmosphere, complete with reverence for the Master and contempt for rival psychologists. This and more personal matters involving my respect for leaders of the organization resulted in a great deal of turmoil on my part. As I could not dispel my doubts, I started to wonder whether to continue or withdraw from the Institute. Having heard about the situation, Jung offered me an interview.

I found him receptive, understanding, and supportive. He listened closely to my mixed feelings about becoming a Jungian, and said, as he had said to others, that he had always been uninterested in gaining disciples. Some people, he observed, seemed to find fulfillment in following his lead, but he had never believed that everyone would be so inclined. He was not in the least defensive about his theories or techniques, encouraging me instead to follow my own path, wherever it might take me. He told me about the rupture in his relations with Freud and how much it had cost him, emotionally, to find his bearings. I was and remain grateful to him for helping me decide to pursue lines of thought more congenial to my nature, but I must report that I did not come to that decision during our interview.

When I left, I was still in a state of conflict, impressed with the man and heartened by our meeting, but entirely unclear as to what "my own path" might be. That very night, however, I had a dream that finally enabled me to resolve the issue. I dreamed that I was on a ship in a dangerously stormy sea. The waves were so high that they threatened to engulf the vessel, and I was hanging on for dear life. Then, at the height of the storm, a voice spoke from Heaven. In resounding tones, it said, "The ship is bound for Providence."

That was all—but I awoke bathed in sweat and tears, terribly shaken but feeling that the answer to my dilemma lay in that cryptic utterance. Thinking about it later that day, I felt that the storm-tossed ship represented the crisis I was in and came to the conclusion that Providence meant both the promised land and Providence, Rhode Island. Since my conflict had come down to remaining in Switzerland or returning to America, I decided that the guiding voice of my unconscious—the Self, if you will—was telling me that my promised land was back home. Without further ado, I announced my intention to leave the Institute.

To this day, I do not know if my interpretation was correct, but it has long ceased to matter. I have never regretted my decision, and it has pleased me mightily to contemplate the irony in this sequence of events. Not only Jung himself, but a most Jungian dream enabled me to see that I was not meant to be a Jungian. It was shortly after that crisis, by the way, that I became seriously interested in the psychology of humor, although at the time I did not see the connection. In any case, my meeting with Jung left me convinced that, whatever he had been and done during his long lifetime, in his old age he was highly capable of being the Wise Old Man, serene and philosophical, objective, modest, and generous.[9]

Where does that leave us with regard to my thesis? I would like to say QED, and let it go at that, but at the risk of redundancy, let me try to sum up the gist of this chapter.

Personality theories are maps of the mind. Since there is no such thing as *the* mind, however, but only *minds* that resemble and differ from each other in many ways, all such theories are necessarily composed of generalizations that their creators think are true. What convinces each one that his map is especially illuminating is first and foremost that it has illuminated his own experience.

In the cases of both Freud and Jung, it should be abundantly clear by now, their theories were eloquent expressions of their selves, their images of human nature based on the nature of the person each of them knew best. That their insights into their own characteristics and therefore into the characteristics of others were profound is not in question, but their profundity must not blind us to the fact that their views were substantially different—antagonistic and irreconcilable on the issues of sexuality and spirituality—because their creators were different. Sigmund Freud and C. G. Jung grew up in diverse cultures, their families exerted discrepant influences on them, and they each found their salvation in different kinds of belief systems. That they did their best to impart these belief systems and their attendant practices[10] to the rest of the world is to their credit and our benefit. That they did not explicitly acknowledge the relativity of their findings, however, and allowed their disciples to transform their theories into dogma, was a shortcoming in these otherwise brilliant men. This shortcoming, I think, was embedded in their personal identification with their teachings, for having the world accept their ideas was tantamount to having it validate themselves.

Having said as much, I want to add that the fact that a theorist's projections of his characteristics onto the face of humanity can enlighten humanity about its unrecognized qualities is, to my mind at least, awe-inspiring. What we see here, I believe, is the miracle of creativity, in the sense that a conflicted human being, struggling to clarify personal confusion, may produce pearls of wisdom from which everyone can benefit.

The pattern I have outlined is as true of other theorists as it was of Freud and Jung. I do not know if it is true of all; but if we took the time, we could uncover it in the cases of Adler, Rank, Reich, Horney, Fromm, and many more contributors to the making of psychology.

What I now propose to do, however, is turn our sights on a leader who specifically eschewed the construction of a personality theory, in order to show that even here it was his own characteristics that led him to adopt a position that succeeded in revolutionizing the field.

1. When Freud and Jung visited this country in 1909 to deliver a series of lectures at Clark University, a leading newspaper reported the event by declaring, "Psychoanalysis can be summed up in one word—filth!"

2. possibly twice, the evidence is unclear (for further details, see Roazen and/or Clark).

3. Only Wilhelm Reich thought he did not carry them far enough. to Reich's mind, the logical extension of Freudian thought was the promotion of free love and the idea that total sexual release would cure all neurotic problems.

4. "Spread out thy wings, Lord Jesus mild/ And take to thee thy chick, thy child./ If Satan would devour it/ No harm shall overpower it/ So let the angels sing!"

5. See *A Secret Symmetry*, by Aldo Carotenuto, Pantheon, 1948, for an account of his affair with Sabina Spielrein, later to become a psychiatrist in her own right.

6. They first appear in clear form in *Symbols of Transformation* (1912) and *On the Psychology of the Unconscious* (1917).

7. One of Jung's fullest discourses on the Self is to be found in *Answer to Job*, 1952.

8. For a book-length expression of this point of view, see Laurens van der Post, *Jung and the Story of Our Time*, Vintage Books, 1977.

9. There was an amusing part to our interview that I might as well confess here, too. We had talked for about 2 hours, but as he was showing me to the door, he said, "Now is there anything else you would like to ask me?" I was twenty-eight and without much grace, so I replied, "Yes, I would like to know more about your relationship with Toni Wolff. *They say* you had a very intimate involvement with her." Jung eyed me thoughtfully for a moment, then murmured, "They say many things," and ushered me out. In retrospect, I thought with some embarrassment, what chutzpah on my part, and what aplomb on his! But that too, perhaps, is one of the things I had to come to learn.

10. As far as practices are concerned, it should be noted that the Jungian techniques of unconscious painting and active imagination both arose from Jung's efforts to heal himself. After the break with Freud, he has said, he was in a "state of disorientation" so great as to make him fear for his sanity. It took almost four years of self-analysis for him to regain his stability, but in the process he created these methods of helping others in the grip of powerful unconscious forces (see *Memories, Dreams, Reflections*, 1961, pp. 170–199).

# 5

# *The Denial of Personality*

B. F. Skinner was born in 1904 in Susquehanna, Pennsylvania. He begins his autobiography:

> The Susquehanna River, named for an Iroquois tribe, rises in Otsego Lake in New York State. It flows southwest and south and crosses into Pennsylvania a few miles below the town of Windsor. Almost at once it meets a foothill of the Alleghenies, which proves unreachable, and it abandons its southern course, swings west and north, and returns to the hospitable plains of New York State. It flows west past Binghamton and Oswego and tackles Pennsylvania again at a more vulnerable point. This time it succeeds and, picking up the support of a large western branch, continues south past the state capital of Harrisburg and into Maryland and Chesapeake Bay, and so at last into the Atlantic Ocean.
>
> In that first attack on Pennsylvania the river has cut a deep sickle-shaped valley about fifteen miles long. The left bank, the outside of the curve, presses tightly against that foothill of the Alleghenies, and the right bank has little land flat enough to be worth farming, but it was once all part of a great hardwood forest, and lumbermen and trappers came, and five towns sprang up within that fifteen-

mile stretch—Lanesboro and Hallstead on the left, named for early settlers, and Oakland, Hickory Grove, and Great Bend on the right, named for two of the most valuable hardwoods and the arc of the river itself. In that narrow sweep of a river valley I spent the first eighteen years of my life.

## THE PERSONALITY THAT DENIES PERSONALITY

This objective, circumstantial description of the physical environment in which he lived is characteristic of the man. In the rest of this volume (*Particulars of My Life,* 1976) and the two that were to follow (*The Shaping of a Behaviorist* and *A Matter of Consequences*), comprising altogether over a thousand pages of reminiscences, Skinner provides a meticulous account of his personal and professional life. He dwells in great detail on his grandparents, parents, and other relatives, his friends and colleagues, adversaries and critics. He describes his various homes and offices, laboratories and studies. He is almost embarrassingly frank about his awkward sexual development and the girls and women he loved. With disarming candor, he relates all the criticism he has endured at the hands of such luminous contemporaries as Margaret Mead, Julian Huxley, Karl Popper, Noam Chomsky, and Carl Rogers. With equal candor, he reveals his driving ambition to "make over the field (of psychology) to suit myself." At no point, however, does his emphasis shift from external to internal, from the outer man to the inner man, from his words and deeds to his feelings and fantasies.

In almost total contrast to Jung and Freud, Skinner has nothing to say about his unconscious and the few remarks he makes about his personality are sketchy and unsophisticated. "In December 1933, Professor Walter Miles gave several paper-and-pencil tests to those who were curious about their personalities. I took them, and a month or two later learned that I had better judgment than 95 percent of the others in the group, was more extroverted than 57 percent, and was more readily annoyed than 65 percent . . . Other evidences of my personality, closer to daily life, were less reassuring. A young woman who typed manuscripts for me said that I had a reputation for conceit . . . I was shaken.

Conceit had been my father's problem, and my mother's coun-
tercontrolling measures had reached me as well" (*Shaping,* 1979,
p. 139).

When a colleague, Anne Roe, attempted to give him the Rorschach and TAT, he reports, "I responded so rapidly to the Rorschach cards that she could not keep up with me, but I could say
nothing at all on Harry Murray's Thematic Apperception Test,
evidently because I had been involved in its construction and knew
what it was said to reveal" (*Consequences,* 1983, p. 31).

Skinner is adept at finding ways to conceal his psychodynamics, perhaps because to reveal them would be embarrassing
to a psychologist who claims such factors are unimportant. In the
epilogue to his autobiography, he says, "I do not believe that my
life shows a type of personality à la Freud, an archetypal pattern
à la Jung, or a schedule of development à la Erikson. There have
been a few abiding themes, but they can be traced to environmental sources rather than to traits of character" (*Consequences,*
1983, p. 401). In other words, in describing himself, Skinner remains consistent with his stance in the field: he eschews acknowl-
edgment of his personality traits beyond the most cursory remarks,
and hopes to present himself convincingly as a creature of circumstance and nothing more.

The attempt is glaringly unsuccessful. Despite his disclaimers,
Skinner's account of his life and work reveals a man whose character traits were instrumental in determining his contribution to
the field. He was no less distinctive a personality than Freud,
Jung, Wundt, or James, and he does not have to affirm his personal
characteristics for us to recognize them. They are visible both in
the ways he has conducted his life and in the arguments he has
put forth in support of his professional position. Above all, his
central conflicts and the manner in which he resolved them underlie his supposedly antitheoretical outlook.

In his own words, referring to a crisis involving a loss of self-
confidence in his youth, "I was floundering in a stormy sea and
perilously close to drowning, but help was on the way" (*Particulars,* 1976, p. 298). That help was "behaviorism and its episte-
mological implications" (*Particulars,* 1976, p. 298). How the behaviorist image of humanity became Skinner's salvation and how
that dynamic, in turn, kept him as fanatically devoted to it as has

been the case throughout his life is central to my thesis. Let me lead up to it, however, by allowing the relevant facts to speak for themselves.

## SKINNER'S BACKGROUND AND PERSONAL DEVELOPMENT

Skinner's family were God-fearing Presbyterians and even more ardent Republicans. His father was of the school that fervently believed FDR would lead this country straight to hell. Fred, as his family called him (the "B" in the "B. F." stands for Burrhus, his mother's maiden name), had one brother, 2 years younger, who died suddenly in his late teens of a massive cerebral hemhorrhage. His death, so senseless and unexpected, had a devastating effect on their parents, but Skinner says, "I submitted to that tragic loss with little or no struggle. At one moment on a fair Sunday morning I was telling my brother about my college experiences . . . and fifteen minutes later he was dead. There was nothing I could do. . . They told my father that my objectivity was helpful . . . but I was far from unmoved" (*Particulars,* 1976, pp. 209–10). This quality of unusual objectivity covering deep but buried emotion is one we will meet with again and again. Fred was and remained throughout his life an unusually cool though intense individual, a man of the strongest convictions, and occasional eruptions of passion, who sustained an unruffled, calm, supremely intellectual demeanor.

Regarding his father, an essentially self-taught attorney who was fairly successful in his profession but felt like a failure all his life, Skinner writes, "He never learned to get along easily with other people. He often appeared conceited and was called 'bumpy,' and I once heard another boy, borrowing the phrase from his parents, refer to my father as 'Big I and little u.' That reputation haunted him all his life, but he never stopped trying to live it down and to be hail-fellow-well-met" (*Particulars,* 1976, p. 11). He traces his father's problems to the influence of his grandmother, and in a touching passage says, "Life was to abrade him, to wear him down. He struggled to satisfy that craving for a sense of worth with which his mother had damned him, but forty years later he would throw himself on his bed, weeping, and cry, 'I am no good, I am no good' " (*Particulars,* 1976, p. 38).

Fred's mother, in contrast, was talented, attractive, and dominant. "She had long chestnut hair and was rated something of a beauty. She was popular. . . . She played the piano in an orchestra and accompanied singers in recitals, and she herself had a lovely contralto voice" (p. 18). "She was proud of her appearance. She stood up for twenty minutes after every meal to preserve her figure, and did indeed keep a good figure and posture all her life. . . . She laughed a good deal and often had uncontrollable giggling spells, but she tended to laugh *at* people. . . . What she found funny was very much like what she knew was not 'right.' She could sit in a railway station and be amused by the odd people she saw, but the same shortcomings in those who were close to her were treated as almost sinful. A shirt and tie which did not go well together were amusing on a stranger; on a son they brought a violent protest. . . . My mother was in many ways the dominant member of the family. She had *consented* to marry my father, and there was an element of consent in her behavior with respect to him throughout his life. . . . She was apparently frigid. . . . She apparently gave my father very little sexual satisfaction. . . . A friend once said that, 'Will Skinner would be a better man if he went to see the chippies now and then' " (pp. 43–5).

Brought up in this household, Fred was taught "to fear God, the police, and what people will think" (*Consequences,* 1983, p. 402). He retained the conservatism of his family with regard to his manner of dress and outward public behavior, but broke with their religious teaching during adolescence. "I remember one incident in that period: ashamed of myself for being afraid of a God I did not believe in I went about saying to myself, 'God damn Jesus Christ, God damn Jesus Christ' " (*Particulars,* 1976, p. 61).

On the whole, however, he remained a good boy, given to occasional pranks, but industrious, studious, reliable, and well-mannered. Both parents held him in high regard, though his father grew jealous of the bond between Fred and his mother. When Skinner was studying at Harvard, he recalls, "My mother was worrying about her health, and she came to Boston to be examined at the Lahey Clinic. She stayed in a hotel near the clinic and, of course, I spent some time with her. She had once told me, giggling, that she thought my father was jealous of her attentions to me, and when she went back to Scranton there seemed to be no doubt about it. She started to tell him all about her trip but when she said, 'Frederic gave me all the attention I could have asked for,' he stopped her and would not hear any more of the story'' (*Shaping*, 1979, pp. 101–2).

While this particular memory may suggest a bit of an Oedipus complex, the problem does not seem to have dogged him to any significant extent. He was, he tells us, extraordinarily innocent about sex, but began to be attracted to girls in his teens and fell in love with nine or ten young women before he met and married Yvonne (Eve) Blue in his early thirties. He describes his awkward sexual explorations in vivid detail, leaving no doubt that he not only found the physical sensations exciting but that he suffered the agonies of unrequited love as acutely as the most romantic of young men.

> The big love of my high-school days was . . . Margaret Persons. She was a tall, willowy redhead who so obviously enjoyed life that it was a pleasure just to watch her. . . . I took her to parties and dances and walked her home afterward. We would stand leaning against a tree in front of her house. We embraced tightly but our hands did not move about, and we kissed but it was not what was then called 'soul' or 'French' kissing. It was enough for both of us just to be together. . . . In the end it was sex that broke us up. I became more sophisticated and one afternoon when we were sitting on the bank of the river near Canavan's Glen I put my hand on her leg for the first time. She stopped me, and we embarked upon a long argument, at the end of which she seemed to capitulate. She said she would let me do what I wanted, but she added that she would then kill herself by jumping into the river, because she could never face her mother again. I was stunned and never made any further advances. (*Particulars*, 1976, p. 169)

> During my first year as a Junior Fellow I met Nedda, who had come to Harvard for graduate studies. She was younger than I by four or five years, but we liked each other immediately and after a date or two we made love. She cooked delicious meals, and I took her to the Boston Symphony and the theater. I fell very much in love with her, but I did not see much of her friends or have much in common with them. After two or three months it was clear

that I was not really a part of her intellectual or social life. One evening I took her out to dinner and she told me that we should break it off. She had been more or less engaged to a young man who was chronically ill, and she was going back to him. It was a reasonable decision, but it hit me hard. As we walked back to her apartment from the subway, I found myself moving very slowly. It was not a pose; I simply could not move faster. For a week I was in almost physical pain, and one day bent a wire in the shape of an N, heated it in a Bunsen burner, and branded my left arm. The brand remained clear for years. (*Shaping*, 1979, p. 137)

These passages not only convey the quality of Skinner's early love life, but contribute to the picture of his developing character structure. Not at all immune to intense romantic longing—there were at least half a dozen young women who broke his heart and left him "in almost physical pain"—when he finally married, he appears to have put that part of life under wraps. He makes no reference to emotional ups and downs in his relations with his wife, nor certainly to any extramarital impulses or affairs. In a manner not uncommon to ambitious, hardworking men of his era, he was devoted to his family (Eve and he were to have two daughters, Julie and Debbie) but even more devoted to his profession. From the time he became a graduate student in psychology, Fred focused more and more of his energy on promoting the cause of behaviorism, until, like Freud and psychoanalysis, it became the very meaning of his life.

## THE DARK YEAR IN SCRANTON

To understand the fascination this school of thought held for Skinner, however, we must go back to when he first encountered it, to a time in his early twenties that he came to call "my Dark Year in Scranton." Shortly before he began his undergraduate residency at Hamilton College, Fred's family had moved to Scranton, where his father had acquired an improved position in his profession. Fred, meanwhile, had begun to be interested in literature, and as a college student he fancied himself a writer. He turned out poems and short stories, wrote a three-act play in a single day ("It was very close to automatic writing and I was not to experience anything like it again for many years"), and eventually met Robert Frost while attending the Summer School of English at Bread Loaf, Vermont.

Frost read some of his fiction and wrote him an encouraging letter. "I ought to say you have the touch of art. The work is clean run. You are worth twice anyone else I have seen in prose this year" (*Particulars*, 1976, p. 249). As a result, the young man asked his parents to support him for one year after graduation, during which time he would write a novel. His father replied with a long letter outlining the importance of finding a practical occupation, but agreed to support him nonetheless. According to plan, therefore, Fred furnished a study and settled down to produce a work of art. To his dismay, however, he found himself blocked and frustrated.

"To all external appearances," he recalls, "I was a writer. But nothing happened. Anything as ambitious as a novel was out of the question. I wrote or started to write a few short stories like those I had sent to Frost, but I finished only one or two of them. . . . The truth was, I had no reason to write anything. I had nothing to say, and nothing about my life was making any change in that condition" (*Particulars*, 1976, pp. 263–4).

In a futile effort to divert himself, Fred studied drawing, practiced the piano and the saxaphone, built ship models, (he had always been ingenious in constructing models and devices of various kinds), and went to parties. Nevertheless, he remained restless and unanchored. Increasingly depressed, he began to feel, for the first and perhaps the only time in his life, that he was a failure. Having persuaded his parents, against their better judgment, that he had a future in fiction, he had been brought to the realization that he was grossly mistaken.

It was there and then, we learn from Skinner's own words, that he adopted the point of view he was to propound for the rest of his life—a point of view that shifts responsibility for a person's behavior from one's self to the environment. "I had apparently failed as a writer of fiction," he says, "but was it not possible that literature had failed me as a method?. . . . Literature as an art form was dead; I would turn to science" (*Particulars*, p. 291).

Psychodynamic psychologists have a name for such a maneuver; it is called *projection*, for it involves the projecting of one's own inner characteristics—especially those one cannot tolerate—onto others (or in Skinner's case, onto imaginative writing in general). As the years since he took this position have demonstrated, literature as an art form was certainly not dead, but it was clearly not viable for Skinner. Rather than assume responsibility for his limitation, however, he chose to denigrate the act of creative writing in general and to ally himself with a school of thought that denied the very existence of the "inner man." "At times," he recalls, "I was quite violent; literature must be demolished" (*Particulars*, 1976, p. 292). The intensity of such a sentiment simply underscores the desperation out of which Fred was constructing his newfound defense system.

A scholarly magazine, *The Dial*, had published some articles by Bertrand Russell which led the struggling young man to Russell's book, *Philosophy*, in which the philosopher devoted a good deal of time to John Watson's *Behaviorism*. . . . "Inspired by Russell," says Skinner, "I bought Watson's *Behaviorism*. When a book by Louis Berman, an endocrinologist, appeared under the title *The Religion Called Behaviorism*, I took up the cudgels and wrote a review which I sent to the *Saturday Review of Literature*. They did not publish it, but in writing it I was more or less defining myself for the first time as a behaviorist" (*Particulars*, 1976, p. 299).

Later that year, 1927, an article by H. G. Wells confirmed Fred's decision to abandon literature and turn to behaviorism as the guiding principle of his life. In the article, Wells compared the value of the contributions to society of Ivan Pavlov, the Russian physiologist and discoverer of the "conditioned reflex," versus those of George Bernard Shaw, the consummate literary figure of the day. He concluded by stating that if both of them were drowning simultaneously on two sides of a pier and he had only one life belt with which to help, he would unhesitatingly throw it to Pavlov. Adds Skinner, "And why should *I* hesitate? There was no reason at all. It was to be graduate study in *psychology*" (*Particulars*, 1976, p. 301)—which really meant in behaviorism, for he had little interest in any other form of psychology and, as he disarmingly confesses, took pains to avoid learning about the rest of the field.

The following fall, Fred enrolled at Harvard. Recalling that time, he says, "I had come to Harvard not because I was a fully committed convert to psychology, but because I was escaping from an intolerable alternative" (*Shaping,* p. 37). From the start, his guiding ambition was to conduct experiments to validate the behaviorist position. Watson, in a manifesto entitled, "Psychology as the Behaviorist Views It" (1913), had already enunciated the credo: "Do away with introspection! Psychology must be objective! Most human behavior can be explained on the basis of conditioning! Psychologists should study the behavior of simple animals, from which all necessary principles can be derived to apply to human beings! The goal of psychology is not the understanding of experience but the prediction and control of behavior!"

Pavlov had shown that dogs could be conditioned to respond to a stimulus (e.g., to salivate to the ringing of a bell) by pairing it with another stimulus (e.g., food) to which they would instinctively respond, and Watson, in his "little Albert" experiment, had shown that a human infant could be similarly conditioned. Now it would be up to Skinner to enlarge upon their work and see how far this line of investigation could lead.

In December of his first year at Harvard, he had written, "I have almost gone over to physiology, which I find fascinating. But my fundamental interests lie in the field of psychology, and I shall probably continue therein, even, if necessary, by making over the entire field to suit myself" (*Shaping,* 1979, p. 38). A few months later, he recalls, "Now it was May again and although I had not made over the entire field, I had composed a segment in which I began to be almost unbearably excited. Everything I touched suggested new and promising things to do. I slept well at night, but my days were feverishly active . . . I thought constantly of my rats, designing new pieces of equipment, and formulating new questions to be answered" (p. 38).

By the following year he had written his parents, "The greatest birthday present I got was some remarkable results from the data of my experiment. . . . In a word, I have demonstrated that the rate in which a rat eats food, over a period of two hours, is a square function of the time. In other words, what was heretofore supposed to be 'free' behavior on the part of the rat is now shown to be just as much subject to natural law as, for example, the rate of his pulse" (p. 59).

To discover and prove that so-called free behavior in rats is really a function of an external condition might be exciting to anyone; but to Skinner the hope that this would lead to proof that free will and conscious (or unconscious) choice in human beings were no less the results of external conditions was what a later generation would call "mind-blowing." He was as gripped by the possibilities of his experiments as any inspired genius, and the drive—or compulsion—to extend the behaviorist view to the very limits of its applicability was never to diminish.

## THE COMPLETE BEHAVIORIST

Still a student at Harvard, he recalls, "I was now so much the complete behaviorist that I was shocked when people I admired used mentalistic terms. When Percy Saunders came to Cambridge, I brought him to Boylston Hall. Watching one of my squirrels running the squirrel cage, he chuckled and said, 'He likes that,' and I was shaken . . . I had trouble with my own speech, catching myself as I started to say 'mind' or 'think,' like an atheist who finds himself saying, 'Thank God' " (p. 80).

These passages begin to suggest what was soon to be palpably clear to everyone who knew him. Fred Skinner, from the moment he entered graduate school, had mapped out his lifework and become invested in it with the zeal of a world reformer. The young man who had objected so strenuously to Berman's book, *The Religion Called Behaviorism,* was already demonstrating the validity of one of that book's contentions—that behaviorism could become a belief system generating the exclusivity, dogma, and righteousness of any other creed.

Skinner's first public declamation of the world-saving power of behaviorism is contained in his Utopian novel, *Walden Two* (1948). A fuller exposition of his views on the future of the human race is put forth in *Beyond Freedom and Dignity* (1971). These two works form the basis for my description of his image of humanity. Before I discuss them, however, let me review the central concept—operant conditioning—for which he is best known, and describe some ingenious devices he invented that brought him first the acclaim of his colleagues, then the attention of the nation.

Operant conditioning differs from classical, or Pavlovian, conditioning in the following manner. In classical conditioning, a passive organism is trained to respond to a stimulus in a way it would not do naturally by pairing that stimulus with one to which the organism has a natural or instinctive response. Thus, in Pavlov's initial experiments, dogs were conditioned to salivate to the sound of a bell by pairing the bell with the presentation of food to the hungry animals. In operant conditioning, on the other hand, an active organism is reinforced for performing certain acts by receiving an immediate reward. Thus, in Skinner's lab, a rat received food pellets for pawing a lever in its cage, while a pigeon received birdseed for raising and moving its head in a certain direction. In *Science and Human Behavior* (1953), Skinner says,

The statement that the bird "learns it will get food by stretching its neck" is an inaccurate report of what has happened. To say that it has acquired the "habit" of stretching its neck is merely a resort to an explanatory fiction, since our only evidence of the habit is the acquired tendency to perform the act. The barest possible statement of the process is this: we make a given consequence contingent upon certain physical properties of behavior (the upward movement of the head), and the behavior is then observed to increase in frequency. . .

A response which has already occurred cannot, of course, be predicted or controlled. We can only predict that similar responses will occur in the future. The unit of a predictive science is, therefore, not a response but a class of responses. The word "operant" will be used to describe this class. The term emphasizes the fact that the behavior *operates* upon the environment to generate consequences. . .

While we are awake, we act upon the environment constantly, and many of the consequences of our actions are reinforcing. Through operant conditioning the environment builds the basic repertoire with which we keep our balance, walk, play games, handle instruments and tools, talk, write, sail a boat, drive a car, or fly a plane. A change in the environment—a new car, a new friend, a new field of interest, a new job, a new location—may find us unprepared, but our behavior usually adjusts quickly as we acquire new responses and discard old. . . (pp. 64–66)

The questions that interest clinicians—why behavior that does *not* appear to be reinforcing, at least in the sense of generating pleasurable consequences, often persists in human beings for years, and the differential issue of why *some* of us adjust to changes in our environment while others do not—are not addressed here; but it should be clear that Skinner considers operant conditioning the prototype for most of the learning we do in our lives.

As far as his inventions are concerned, the device that came to be known as the "Skinner box" was the first to generate attention from his colleagues. It is simply an enclosure in which an experimental animal (e.g., a rat) can be housed, containing nothing but a water dish, a lever that controls the food supply, and a delivery chute for food pellets. Outside the box, however, is a mechanism for recording the intervals at which the rat paws the lever, as well as one that can be set to deliver food on any schedule the experimenter wishes to try. Since the unit functions automatically, the rat's behavior can be recorded 24 hours a day, and the strength of conditioning under various schedules of reinforcement (e.g. a food pellet delivered every time the rat paws the lever, every fifth time, in a haphazard pattern, etc.) can be studied and compared.

The simplicity and elegance of the device, combined with the broad implications for human behavior that Skinner was ingenious enough to infer, brought him to the forefront of psychology quite early in his career. By the time he was in his forties, psychologists in the know were referring to him as a future leader of the field.

During World War II, Skinner conducted a series of experiments in which he trained sets of pigeons to navigate bombs dropped from aircraft so they would hit their targets accurately. The pigeons were to be harnessed inside the nose cones of the bombs, with a screen in front of them on which was projected the visual image of the target. They had been trained, through operant conditioning, to keep their eyes on such images by moving their heads slightly to keep the image in view. Attached to their heads were rods whose movements steered the bombs.

Bizarre as it sounds, the experiment apparently worked, and Skinner was eventually able to interest the army brass in observing a demonstration. The operation became known as "Project Pigeon" and was classified until the end of the war. It was never used, however, partly because the officers who considered it found it ludicrous, but also because by this time the U.S. was preparing to launch the atom bomb.

An item of greater interest to the public was designed by Skinner to help his wife and himself raise their second child, Debbie. He called it the "baby-tender" and spent years trying to distribute it commercially. He described it as a "crib-sized living space" that had "sound-absorbing walls and a large picture window. Air entered through filters at the bottom and, after being warmed and moistened, moved upward through and around the edges of a tightly stretched canvas, which served as a mattress. A strip of sheeting ten yards long passed over the canvas, a clean section of which could be cranked into place in a few seconds. . . . When Debbie came home, she went directly into this comfortable space and began to enjoy its advantages. She wore only a diaper. Completely free to move about, she was soon pushing up, rolling over, and crawling. She breathed warm, moist, filtered air, and her skin was never waterlogged with sweat or urine. Loud noises were muffled (though we could hear her from any part of the house). And a curtain pulled over the window shielded her from bright light when she was sleeping" (*Shaping,* 1979, pp.275–6).

Skinner's arguments in favor of the baby tender involved the fact that the danger of an infant smothering in its bedclothes was eliminated, that the baby enjoyed more protection from infection than would ordinarily be the case, and that a controlled environment was preferable to the environment of most households in which children are raised. He saw no disadvantage in the fact that body contact and handling of the child by its parents were severely reduced, nor certainly in the infant's isolation from its parents' moods and emotions.

The rest of the nation did not, by and large, agree with him. While a few hundred models were sold and some of his close friends used the device, most people seemed to feel it was unnatural to keep their infants in such enclosures, so the baby tender was never successfully marketed.

Years later, with his academic reputation firmly established, Skinner had more success in initiating programmed instruction and the use of teaching machines in school settings. He invented the first of these devices also to help his daughters, but went on to promote the principle that mechanical and electronic "teachers" were more reliable and effective than human ones—a stand that won him both acclaim and opposition in educational circles.

In encountering criticism of his ideas, Skinner appears to have been unshaken. He cites such eminent opponents of his views as Julian Huxley, Karl Popper, Eric Fromm, Margaret Mead, Noam Chomsky, and Carl Rogers, but in the face of their strongest attacks, muses, "I was no less convinced that I was right."

At one point, Rogers wrote Skinner, "I don't know any American psychologist today with whom I feel a deeper philosophical disagreement" (*Consequences,* 1983, p. 121). Mead accused him of wanting to play God, Fromm argued that people were essentially different than pigeons, Chomsky said he misunderstood the basic structure of language, and Karl Popper wrote, "Skinner is an enemy of freedom and democracy. He has explained his contempt for freedom quite openly in his book *Beyond Freedom and Dignity*. He has expounded it many years before in a book *Walden Two,* which is the dream of a very kind but megalomaniac behaviorist who defends a behaviorist dictatorship" (p. 391).

Skinner quotes all these critics generously, as he reproduces the following correspondence between himself and Julian Huxley. "I sent a copy of (*Behaviorism at Fifty*) to Julian Huxley, in return for papers he had sent me. In a note I asked myself, 'Do I hope to change him? Not much. But if he is now at least aware of a reasonable alternative view, he may be less outspoken.' With the article I sent a none-too-tactful letter. 'I am always disturbed,' I said, 'when I find a distinguished scientist accepting a dualistic view of the universe.' That was *lese majeste,* and I soon had his answer: 'Thanks for your letter and interesting article. I too am disturbed by distinguished scientists taking dualistic views of the universe. I have always striven to reach a truly monistic or unified view, in which mind and body, both subjective and objective should find a place. I am equally disturbed when I find scientists taking a reductionist point of view and arriving at a spurious monism by disregarding one of the two aspects of reality' " (pp. 238–9).

Rather than feel chastened by these observations, the father of modern behaviorism simply contends that all these scholars were misguided, that they were unable to understand the validity and benefits of his work. Had he remained truer to the tenets of his own position, he might more logically have said that their contingencies of reinforcement had made them prone to uphold their points of view, while his reinforcements had made him inclined to defend his, with the questions of truth and potential benefit to the human race being decidedly secondary as a basis for the controversy.

In any case, *Walden Two* and *Beyond Freedom and Dignity* being the works that won him his widest audiences and brought him the harshest attacks, let us see what they profess.

A Utopian novel set in contemporary America, *Walden Two* is the story of a visit by a small group of academics to an extraordinary community run along strictly behaviorist lines. They are variously impressed and repelled by what they see. The community was founded by a man named Frazier, a former psychologist turned social reformer, whose belief in operant conditioning knows no bounds. He shows *Walden Two* to his visitors—a psychology professor named Burris, a philosophy professor named Castle, and several graduate students—keeping up a running commentary on its virtues, at first in a fairly objective manner, but eventually with all the fervor of a zealot.

At the beginning of their visit, for instance, he takes the group out for a walk. "This is our lawn," he says. "But we consume it. Indirectly, of course—through our sheep. And the advantage is that it doesn't consume us. Have you ever pushed a lawn mower? The stupidest machine ever invented—for one of the stupidest of purposes. But I digress. We solved our problem with a portable electric fence which could be used to move our flock of sheep about the lawn like a gigantic mowing machine. . . . At night the sheep are taken across the brook to the main fold. But we soon found that the sheep kept to the enclosure and quite clear of the fence, which didn't need to be electrified. So we substituted a piece of string, which is easier to move around." "What about the new lambs?" Barbara asked, turning her head at a slight angle and looking at Frazier from the corners of her eyes. "They stray," Frazier conceded, "but they cause no trouble and soon learn to keep with the flock. The curious thing is—you will be interested in this, Burris—the curious thing is that most of these sheep have never been shocked by the fence. Most of them were born after we took the wire away. It has become a tradition among our sheep never to approach string. The lambs acquire it from their elders, whose judgment they never question." "It's fortunate that sheep don't talk," said Castle. "One of them would be sure to ask 'Why?' The Philosophical Lambkin" (*Walden Two*, 1948, pp. 15–16).

The incident seems innocuous enough, but the reader soon learns that it is a prototype for the rest of the story. Not only the animals but also the people at *Walden Two* have been conditioned to be of service to the community and to carry out their appointed duties without complaint and without question. The resultant peacefulness and efficiency of the place becomes captivating to some of the visitors, but it disturbs others, especially Castle, who continually raises the issue of human beings being deprived of their freedom of choice.

Frazier's counterargument, like his author's, is that so-called freedom of choice is an illusion. We are all controlled by our environments, he says. We make continual efforts to control each other—teachers to control their students, students to control their teachers; parents to control their children, children to control their parents; friends and lovers, governments and citizens, all are engaged in this enterprise—but we do it poorly, haphazardly, because we don't understand what we're doing and even refuse to acknowledge the truth of our behavior. *Walden Two* is different from the rest of the world, therefore, primarily in the fact that it is a thoroughly planned society in which the assignment of life-styles to individuals and their being brought up to accept their life-styles as complacently as the grass-mowing sheep is seen as an ultimate good.

Getting carried away near the end of the story, Frazier addresses his guests in a state of mounting excitement. "What remains to be done?" he said, his eyes flashing. "Well, what do you say to the design of personalities? Would that interest you? The control of temperament? Give me the specifications and I'll give you the man! . . . And what about the cultivation of special abilities? Do we know anything about the circumstances in the life of the child which give him a mathematical mind? Or make him musical? Almost nothing at all! These things are left to accident or blamed on heredity. I take a more optimistic view: we can analyze effective behavior and design experiments to discover how to generate it in our youth. Oh, our efforts will seem pretty crude a hundred years hence. They may seem crude now to the expansive soul. But we've got to make a start. There's no virtue in accident. Let us control the lives of our children and see what we can make of them" (*Walden Two,* 1948, pp. 274–5).

Throughout the book, the visitors wrestle with the moral dilemma it presents. Is it right for people to be controlled for their own good, or is our freedom of choice to be protected at all costs? Their opinions are divided, but the most intense struggle takes place in the mind of Professor Burris. Almost to the end, he cannot decide whether to return to his previous life, with all its frustrations and inconsistencies, or to throw in his lot with Frazier and become an inhabitant of Walden Two. He gets as far as the train station in his decision to return, then changes his mind for good.

"On my way out of the station, I passed a telegraph counter. For a fleeting moment I remembered the University. Should I at least serve notice of my defection? I stepped up to the counter, feeling as I sometimes felt after seeing a particularly debonair hero in the movies. I picked up a pencil and began to swing it by its chain, as I considered how to phrase my message . . . I set to work and entered the name and address of the president in expansive block letters. Then, unmindful of standard telegraphic style and struggling to control my euphoric abandon, I printed slowly and with great care: MY DEAR PRESIDENT MITTELBACH STOP YOU MAY TAKE YOUR STUPID UNIVERSITY. . ." (*Walden Two,* 1948, pp. 295–6).

Years later, Skinner wrote, "Much of the life in *Walden Two* was my own at the time. Frazier played the Schumann piano quintet about as well as I did and his relations to the other players were mine to my talented young friends . . . the issues Fraizer discussed with Castle I had discussed with a group of philosophers and literary critics . . . in discussing the implications of a science and technology of behavior with these friends, I took a fairly extreme position—one that I should not always have wanted to defend publicly—but in the book I could go much further. I could enjoy poetic license. I let Frazier say things I myself was not yet ready to say to anyone. . . . Eventually (however) I became a devout Frazierian" (*Shaping*, 1979, pp. 297–8).

While it did not catch on at the time it was published, *Walden Two* was to sell over 2 million copies in years to come. Originally, however, it (and Skinner) were attacked in *Life* Magazine under the heading, "The Newest Utopia is a Slander on Some Old Notions of the Good Life." "In spirit," ran the review, "*Walden Two* is as much like Thoreau's original *Walden* as a Quonset hut is like a . . . Cape Cod house. Dr. Skinner is the professor of psychology who is responsible for the invention of something known as 'the mechanical baby tender' . . . But the menace of the mechanical baby tender is as nothing compared to the menace of books like *Walden Two*. For Dr. Skinner's utopia is a triumph of 'cultural engineering' and 'behavioral engineering' where the conditioned reflex is king. . . . Once they are trained, the inhabitants of *Walden Two* have 'freedom.' But it is the freedom of those Pavlovian dogs which are free to foam at the mouth whenever the 'dinner' bell invites them to a nonforthcoming meal" (pp. 347–8).

Never daunted, Skinner continued to propound his views in a dozen other volumes, including *Science and Human Behavior* (1953), *Cumulative Record* (1959), *The Technology of Teaching* (1968), *Contingencies of Reinforcement* (1969), *Beyond Freedom and Dignity* (1971), and *About Behaviorism* (1974). While they all reiterate the same basic themes, *Beyond Freedom and Dignity* is probably the most specific and certainly the most provocative in presenting Skinner's image of humanity in its present evolutionary quandary.

The title must be taken literally. Skinner lets us know from the outset that he considers the value placed on our so-called freedom to shape our own lives, as well as the vaunted ideal of the dignity of the individual, to be outmoded notions whose time has past. It is his intention to argue them into oblivion. He attacks them by insisting that a "technology of behavior" based on the principles of operant conditioning could produce a world as free from crime, unhappiness, and inefficiency as from our unfortunate overestimation of the worth of the individual and our common delusion that there actually is such a thing as freedom of the will.

"The literature of freedom," he says, "has encouraged escape from or attack upon all controllers. It has done so by making any indication of control aversive. Those who manipulate human behavior are said to be evil men, necessarily bent on exploitation. Control is clearly the opposite of freedom, and if freedom is good, control must be bad. What is overlooked is control which does not have aversive consquences. . . . The problem is to free men, not from control, but from certain kinds of control'' (pp. 38–9).

With regard to dignity, ''We recognize a person's dignity or worth when we give him credit for what he has done. The amount we give is inversely proportional to the conspicuousness of the causes of his behavior. If we do not know why a person acts as he does, we attribute his behavior to him. . . . We admire people to the extent that we cannot explain what they do. . . . What we may call the literature of dignity is concerned with preserving due credit. It may oppose advances in technology, including a technology of behavior, because they destroy chances to be admired and a basic analysis because it offers an alternative explanation of behavior for which the individual himself has previously been given credit'' (p. 55).

Addressing the heart of the matter, whether it is morally justifiable for certain people consciously to set out to control the lives of others, even for their own good, Skinner avers, ''To refuse to control is to leave the control not to the person himself, but to other parts of the environment.''

The human being who emerges from this argument is a creature at the mercy of his surroundings, one who deludes himself into thinking that he has free will, one who further confounds himself by imagining that his so-called inner world of fantasy, feeling, and thought are important, a creature who is inherently neither bad nor good, but who is basically malleable and unfortunately misguided. This creature can be trained to behave in efficient and cooperative ways, but the primary deterrent to this achievement is the creature's belief in its inner self. Once this is eradicated and we accept the argument that we are merely products of our circumstances, we as individuals and our society as a whole will make progress on our collective problems.

Most reviewers of *Beyond Freedom and Dignity* were appalled. Noam Chomsky, in the *New York Review of Books* (Dec. 30, 1971), wrote, ''Skinner confuses 'science' with terminology.

He apparently believes that if he rephrases commonplace 'mentalistic' expressions with terminology derived from the laboratory study of behavior, but deprived of whatever content this terminology has within this discipline, then he has achieved a scientific analysis of behavior. . . . For Skinner's argument to have any force, he must show that people have wills, impulses, feelings, purposes and the like no more than rocks do." Richard Sennett, in the *New York Times Book Review* (Oct. 24, 1971), said, "He appears to understand so little, indeed to care so little, about society itself that the reader comes totally to distrust him," and Walter Arnold, in the *Saturday Review* (Oct. 9, 1971), concluded, "This is one of the strangest amalgams of compassion and misanthropy that has ever been my puzzlement to read. . . . [The book's] most important service is the negative one of providing an example of the absurdity to which the superstition of scientism leads."

Our concern, however, is not so much with the validity or popularity of Skinner's stance as with the factors that made him adopt it in the first place and cling to it as tenaciously as he has throughout his lifetime. To shed light on these issues, we must return to his "Dark Year" in Scranton, for it was then and there that he made the decision that was to shape his professional career.

Alan C. Elms (1981) describes this period in Skinner's life as follows: "During his final undergraduate term, feeling compelled to choose an occupational identity, Skinner decided to become a writer. He had already written extensively for college publications and had participated in the Bread Loaf summer writing school. At the point of making his career choice, he received an encouraging letter from Robert Frost. He subsequently proposed to spend a year at home writing a novel. His father expressed serious reservations about the plan, but offered to support him financially for the year, on the condition that Skinner would 'go to work' if his writing career was not well launched by year's end. Within three months, Skinner was already admitting failure. 'The results were disastrous. I frittered away my time. . .' In his notebook Skinner blamed his parents for 'unwittingly forcing' him into his 'present course' as well as for making fun of his 'effeminate' interests and time-wasting activities. He blamed the city of Scranton, where his family then lived, for being 'ready to quench any ideas of my own I may have. . .' He blamed literature itself for being 'a mean satisfaction of a mean instinct' and for being unable to express the subtleties of life. . . . The Dark Year was dark for several reasons. Not only did Skinner discover that he was unable to write anything important, but he was often the object (or fancied himself to be the object) of jibes and innuendos from people who would have considered even a successful writing career as inappropriate for a healthy young man" (p. 472).

"The Dark Year," Elms concludes, "clearly involved an identity crisis. Most important, Skinner's occupational identity, which had been gradually constructed during college and then confirmed by Frost's letter, abruptly collapsed. Further, Skinner was unable to find in the reactions of others any clear indication that he was a worthy individual. . . . The crisis was finally resolved as such intense identity crises often are: through the wholehearted acceptance of an ideology—indeed an extreme ideology—in Skinner's case, radical behaviorism" (p. 473).

Elms's analysis is apt. To flesh it out, let us first consider the essential differences between a career devoted to writing poetry and fiction and one devoted to promoting the cause of behaviorism. The former requires commitment to such intrapsychic processes as inspiration, intuition, free association, the stream of consciousness, and the participation of the unconscious, as well as considering fantasies and feelings important parts of one's being. The latter denies it all—makes fantasies and feelings, indeed the entire intrapsychic domain, recede into a background of (to use Skinner's favorite term) "pre-scientific" notions, while attention is focused on observable behavior and the operations necessary to record, predict, and control it effectively.

When Skinner chose behaviorism as a lifebuoy in his sea of despair, he chose to validate himself through the exercise of his intellectual, perceptual, and mechanical aptitudes, but his sense of failure as a neophyte writer was so disconcerting that he warded it off by the use of such well-known defense mechanisms as denial, rationalization, and projection. In the final volume of his autobiography, he wrote, "I recovered slowly from my failure as a writer of fiction," and "During the Dark Year in Scranton . . . I was depressed . . . I did not consider actual suicide; behaviorism offered me another way out: It was not I but my history that had failed" (*Consequences,* 1983, p. 407).

"It was not I but my history that had failed." A curious phrase, to say the least, but it contains the crux of Skinner's initial motivation for choosing behaviorism as the flag he was evermore to defend. His inability to accept youthful failure as part of his self-concept—to "own it," in the words of another school of psychology—may have been a reaction to his father's lifelong struggle with the feeling of being a failure and his family's overall emphasis on successful achievement as the hallmark of a worthwhile life; but it fueled his attraction to behaviorism as an explanatory system and his attendant intolerance of rival psychological theories.

Sociologically and interpersonally, the most hotly debated issue Skinner's form of radical behaviorism raises is the value of personal freedom versus control by others. Intrapsychically, however, the issue is one of spontaneity versus restraint and self-control, one of allowing unconscious, intuitive, and emotional elements of oneself to express themselves freely or intellectually controlling and denying their existence in one's psychic economy.

Judging from his autobiography, as well as from his entire *oeuvre,* Fred Skinner experienced youthful struggles with these two sides of himself but came more and more to value control over spontaneity, intellectual processes over emotional ones. Whereas in his teens and twenties he was romantically in love with a series of girls and young women to the extent that he suffered acute pain when they rejected him, and while in his autobiography he confesses, "I weep at movies, when listening to music, or just thinking about someone I love," in the end he boldly declares, "I do not think feelings are important" (*Consequences,* p. 399).

If I were to compose a personality portrait of the great psychologist who spent his life denying that personality portraits are of psychological value, I would describe the adult B. F. Skinner in the following terms:

> He is highly intelligent, astute, and articulate. He is persistent, ambitious, and hardworking. He is mechanically ingenious, practical, objective, and self-controlled, yet a streak of romanticism,

idealism, and sentimentality lives on in him from his youth. He displays a fine sense of humor which he is able to direct at himself as well as at others. He is personally modest but proud of his achievements. From the time of his "failure as a writer of fiction" and subsequent adopting of behaviorism as his creed, he has exhibited an amazing lack of self-doubt in the face of persistent criticism from other leading scholars.

He is a fairly conventional family man whose emotional needs appear to be met by his wife and daughters. His affection for his daughters is substantial. He is entirely out of touch with his unconscious, however, as shown in the fact that he reports not a single dream in a thousand pages of autobiography, as well as in his highly defensive reaction to taking (or almost taking) the Rorschach and TAT. He sees himself, accurately I think, as a product of the Protestant ethic, his mother's admonitions, and a struggle with the problem his father modeled for him—conceit or self-aggrandizement covering a sense of personal inadequacy—but he has handled that problem quite successfully. He was intellectually influenced, he says, by Bacon, Darwin, and John B. Watson, but he is a powerfully original thinker in his own right. The successful achievement of self-control is a key factor in his personality, as are such qualities as rationality, single-mindedness, and resoluteness. He is a highly systematic individual who has tamed, but not obliterated, his impulses, feelings, and fantasies by consistently making them secondary to his intellectual processes.

If I am correct in this assessment, it should not be difficult to see why behaviorism was made to order for Skinner and why he was a perfect person to become its champion. The congruence of his personal traits with the tenets of the system that he helped develop into a leading school of thought is as close as James's congruence with the stream of consciousness, as Jung's identification with the collective unconscious. This does not, however, constitute a criticism of that school's validity or its leader's brilliance.

As a working method, behaviorism has proven itself remarkably effective in many areas of life. It has made significant contributions to the fields of education and psychotherapy, as well as to our understanding of human behavior in general. What the congruence shows is simply the fact that the major promoter of this line of investigation was, despite his denial of psychodynamics and personality theory, bound to make the contributions he has by his psychodynamics and personality traits. It also explains why, for Skinner, behaviorism became not a working method, but a philosophy of life. His very identity is imbedded in it, and was from the start. If the behaviorist doctrine is true, its leader need have no doubts about his own life choices, especially the choice to desert fiction for psychology. If behaviorism can be seriously questioned, on the other hand, the "Dark Year in Scranton" would raise its ugly head yet again.

When *A Matter of Consequences* appeared in 1983, I reviewed it for the *Los Angeles Times*. Skinner, whom I had happened to bump into at an APA convention, asked me to send him a copy of the review. I did so with some trepidation, for, although it said he was "a likable man," it contained the following paragraphs:

He is not above occasional acts of sophomoric maliciousness. "When (Erich Fromm) began to argue that people were not pigeons, I decided that something had to be done. On a scrap of paper, I wrote, 'Watch Fromm's left hand. I am going to shape a chopping motion,' and passed it down the table. . . . He gesticulated a great deal as he talked, and whenever his left hand came up, I looked straight at him. If he brought the hand down, I nodded and smiled. Within five minutes he was chopping the air so vigorously that his wristwatch kept slipping out over his hand." Inconsequential as it may seem, this incident bears on the heart of the matter. Skinnerian psychology can certainly explain and control peripheral behavior, but can it affect the convictions of intelligent people? Could Skinner have pulled any trick that would have changed Fromm's outlook on life? Given appropriate contingencies of reinforcement, could we turn Skinner into a psychoanalyst?

There is much to learn from Skinner's revelations—primarily, that the guiding principle in the great behaviorist is precisely his "inner man." . . . With its exclusive focus on outer conditions, behaviorism provided Skinner with a rationalization for his problems. A psychologist with the soul of an engineer, he is constrained to view the world in an exclusively scientific manner. The stifled artist within him fails to appreciate the momentousness of choice, the thrill of inspiration. "When I played the saxophone in dance orchestras," he recalls, "I read the notes; I could never break free as jazz required." There we have it. In Skinner's world, as in *Wal-*

*den Two,* we would all play the notes set down for us by the behavior controllers. Improvisation would destroy the system.

When I sent him the piece, he replied with a courteous note. "Thanks for sending me the copy of the review. Of course I don't agree with you on your central point, but the review is an honest and decent effort to present my book. Thank you. Yours sincerely, B. F. Skinner."

# 6

# Psychotherapy As An Art Form

Is the practice of psychotherapy a science or an art? This question underlies a set of differences that distinguish practitioners and schools of thought, sometimes making them intolerant of each other's methods and teachings, at other times merely causing them to approach their common task in highly divergent ways.

Those who conceive of therapy as a science are concerned to develop tried-and-true procedures of diagnosis and treatment. They seek for principles that apply to all cases within a defined group, for techniques that can be standardized and used by anyone well enough trained. They have a stake in objectivity as a stance, determinism as a philosophy.

Those who conceive of therapy as an art, on the other hand, see it as an expression of the individuality of the practitioner aimed at exploring and encouraging the individuality of the client. Their approach is ideographic rather than nomothetic, focusing on the uniqueness of each person, rather than on the patterns that run through classes of people or categories of psychopathology. Their methods have something in common with the playing styles of musical artists, in that each is recognizably unique, though they all may be trained in psychology as the performers are trained in music. To use another analogy, their work may be compared to the works of portrait painters, for both strive to capture the individuality of their subjects. They have a stake in sensitive, perceptive subjectivity and nondeterminism, and are inspired by the desire to help their clients "become who they are."

## THERAPY BOTH A SCIENCE AND AN ART

Both the scientific and artistic aspirations of psychotherapists seem defensible to me. At its present stage of development, the practice is still undefined; but my own predilection would be for it to remain forever a combination of science and art. Only the two together seem to do justice to the complexities of human beings struggling with the kinds of issues that bring most people to therapy. In this formulation, however, the more a therapist practices his trade as an art form, the more likely it becomes that his style and techniques of treatment will be colored by personal experience—or to put it more succinctly, the characteristic ways in which such therapists attempt to help others spring directly from whatever helped *them* weather difficult times in their own lives.

Carl Rogers, as we shall see, must be rated among those who have succeeded in furthering both the scientific and artistic goals of the profession. In his dedication to scientific objectivity, he was one of the first to record and publish verbatim transcripts of his sessions. He was also among the first to conduct research studies of the efficacy of his methods. At the same time, in line with the values of therapy as an art, he has consistently defended the principle of the uniqueness of the individual, and has built his entire approach around the goal of helping people discover their own truths and become their genuine selves.

Early in his career, Rogers called his method of therapy "nondirective." He later changed the qualifying adjective to "client-centered," still later to "person-centered," in order to put more emphasis on the positive value of the client taking the lead than on the therapist's refraining from asking questions, giving advice, or otherwise directing the interaction. He developed a distinctive, original style, but the central concept associated with his name has long been "unconditional positive regard." This guiding attitude, with its implications of calm acceptance, nonjudgmental empathy, and faith in the client's ability to work out his own salvation, is as characteristic of Rogers the man as it is of Rogers the clinician. How he came to be this way and why these qualities have been so important to him is part of the substance of this chapter. How he translated them into a method of therapy and why that method became so influential in mid-twentieth century America is another part.

Having shown how my thesis applies to Rogers's approach, I will show how it applies to the equally distinctive but very different approach of Milton Erickson. Since less biographical material has been published on Erickson than on the other figures discussed in this book, my treatment of him will be relatively brief. Nevertheless, the contrast he provides should be illuminating, for it will help establish the point that whatever techniques a gifted therapist originates derive from personal experience, as well as show that that fact is a handicap only to those who believe their techniques should be universally effective.

## CARL ROGERS AND CLIENT-CENTERED COUNSELING

A product of rural midwestern America in the first half of the twentieth century, Carl Rogers can be said to represent the triumph of Christian values in the field of psychotherapy. "I was brought up," he has said, "in a home marked by close family ties, a very strict and uncompromising religious and ethical atmosphere, and what amounted to a worship of the virtue of hard work" (*On Becoming a Person*, 1961, p. 5). Both in his writings and in person, he came across as an industrious, upright individual whose optimistic outlook on human nature was supported by his intelligence and candor. His speech, flat and measured, had a soothing, monotonous quality inducing both calmness and boredom. There was a level-eyed intensity in his face, however, that bespoke much more depth than the surface readily revealed.

And depth there was. Both his character and intellect contained surprising vistas—profundities that help explain the achievement of this remarkable man. As we trace the development of his life and work, we will see them emerge, for we will be witness to a set of subtle but momentous changes through which a boy brought up in a fundamentalist home affirmed his own individuality and forged a therapeutic system by which others could affirm themselves as well.

The fourth child of Julia and Walter Rogers, Carl was born in 1902 in Oak Park, a small town near Chicago. Two brothers and a sister had preceded him; two more brothers were to follow. According to his biographer, Howard Kirschenbaum (1979), "Carl was a rather sickly child—slight, shy, prone to tears, often the target of jokes and teasing by his older brothers. With his father often away from home on business trips, he developed much warmer feelings for his mother. The baby of the family for over five years, he received considerable attention from her and the older children, who taught him to read at about age four. He seemed to take easily to the world of books and before long was reading many of the thick volumes on the family's bookshelves, especially a book of Bible stories . . . which he read from beginning to end many times, to the approval of his religion-minded parents" (pp. 2–3).

Both Walter and Julia Rogers had attended the University of Wisconsin. Walter became a civil engineer and, in time, quite a prosperous man. When Carl was in high school, the family moved to a 300-acre farm, partly because of his parents' interest in agriculture, but also because they believed the move would protect their children against the corrupting influence of city life.

Rogers has described his parents as religious, practical, and anti-intellectual. Their religious and moral standards are the subject of many of his reminiscences. "My mother was a person with strong religious convictions. . . . Two of her biblical phrases, often used in family prayers, stick in my mind and give the feeling of her religion: 'Come out from among them and be ye separate,' and 'All our righteousness is as filthy rags in Thy sight, oh Lord.' " Expanding on this theme, he has said, "I think the attitude toward persons outside our large family can be summed up schematically in this way: 'Other persons behave in dubious ways which we do not approve of in our family. Many of them play cards, go to movies, smoke, dance, drink, and engage in other activities, some unmentionable. So the best thing to do is to be tolerant of them, since they may not know better, but to keep away from any close communication with them, and to live your life within the family.' . . . To the best of my recollection, this unconsciously arrogant separateness characterized my behavior all through elementary school" (*A Way of Being*, 1980, pp. 27–8).

Here as elsewhere, we must be grateful for Rogers's candor. (In my initial interview with him while composing this chapter, he told me that he had once asked his favorite brother what he thought of their mother. "She was a person you didn't tell things to," came the reply, and Rogers said he thought that was accurate.) What he does, on the whole, is recount quite clearly the formative influences on his character. All that remains is to understand their significance.

As I see it, his mother's influence was double-edged. She struggled with a conflict between pride and humility, between seeing her family as more moral than others and reminding herself that in God's eyes we are all pretentious. Very close to her emotionally, appreciating her attentiveness but feeling that he could not trust her because she was too judgmental, her son developed a need to repudiate her narrow-mindedness, while remaining identified with her high moral standards. He was not, however, capable of making the transition until he was past adolescence.

Carl was shy and sensitive as a schoolboy. He had no close friends and was something of a teacher's pet. As an adolescent he became strong and wiry, but in character remained a hardworking, high-minded student. His primary goals were to learn his lessons and prepare himself for a meaningful career. He had but one date during high school, taking a girl to an event he was forced to attend, and engaged in no intimate contact with the opposite sex until he was in his twenties.

Carl entered the University of Wisconsin at the age of seventeen, majoring in scientific agriculture. An interest in science vied in his mind with the religious aspirations that had been instilled in him. We may ascribe this interest, I think, to his father's example. As a civil engineer and a modern farmer, the elder Rogers had frequently shown his son the value of objective research and had rewarded him both verbally and materially when Carl pursued such activities on his own.

As Kirschenbaum reports, "Because Walter Rogers wanted to run the farm in the most modern way, he frequently had experts from the university out to advise him . . . about the best methods. Carl often listened to these experts but, at first, had little interest in the subject. Then he began to read many of his father's books, magazines, and catalogues on farming. . . . Later he recalled, 'I can remember reading these books—particularly the heavy scientific one by Morison on Feeds and Feeding. The descriptions of all the scientific experiments . . . gave me a thoroughgoing feeling for the essential elements of science. The design of a suitable experiment, the rationale of control groups, the control of all variables but one, the statistical analysis of the results—all these concepts were unknowingly absorbed through my reading at the age of 13 to 16' " (p. 14).

With regard to his inner life during adolescence, Rogers has said, "My fantasies during this period were definitely bizarre, and probably would be classed as schizoid by a diagnostician, but fortunately I never came in contact with a psychologist" (*A Way of Being*, 1980, p. 30).

What he did come in contact with was the Christian youth movement. He lived at the campus YMCA and became an active participant in Christian Fellowship. That this was not merely a form of social activity but touched him at his core seems apparent from letters he wrote at the time. "I have just come from a fine fellowship meeting. 'Dad' Wolfe spoke on 'Selecting a Lifework.' Oh, it's wonderful to feel that God will really lead me to my life-work, and I know He will, for never has He deserted me . . . I have plenty of ambition, in fact sometimes I think I'm too ambitious, but if I can only keep that terrible swelling force within me in the right path, I know all will be well" (Kirschenbaum, 1979, p. 20). And, "During Eddy's morning speech I almost made up my mind to go into Christian work and during his afternoon speech I made my final decision. God help me keep it! All my previous dreams seem cheap now, for I have volunteered for the biggest, the greatest work on the globe" (p. 21).

A Freudian interpretation would probably designate that "terrible swelling force" as a phallic symbol, and it may well be that Carl's passion for Christian work was fueled by sublimated sexual energy; but we must not forget that his entire upbringing had emphasized the virtues of Christianity. In any case, for the next few years, he aimed in the direction of the ministry as his vocation.

To his great good fortune, at age nineteen Carl was chosen to be one of 10 U.S. youth delegates to the World Student Christian Federation Conference in Peking. As a result, he spent 6 months in China, observing and discoursing with people from many parts of the world.

The experience had a profound effect on the eager, bright, but, until now, provincial young man. To begin with, it opened his eyes to the exploitation of human beings practiced in the name of good business. "Visiting a Chinese silk factory, he saw six- and seven-year-old girls . . . working over tubs of steaming water all day long. 'Somehow silk will never look the same to me (he wrote). It has lost considerable of its luster. . . . Anyone who could see those tiny little kids (some of the poor little tykes were just having their feet bound and stood first on one foot and then on the other to ease the pain)—anyone who could see those little kids, and say that such things were all right, is not a Christian, by my definition. I don't care whether he believes the whole Bible from beginning to end or whether he believes every orthodox doctrine that ever was—I couldn't call him a Christian' " (Kirschenbaum, 1979, p. 28).

At the same time, Carl's contact with intellectually stimulating companions liberalized his religious views to an extent that would be decisive for his future. Christ, he came to believe, was not a deity but "a man who came nearer to God than any other man in history." Devout as that statement may sound to many today, to his fundamentalist parents it was heretical. Their son, they knew, had begun to question their rigid belief system several years before, but now he had made it clear that he was adopting a different—though still Christian-oriented—stance. His letters home let them know he was seeing the world from a brand new perspective. The shift unnerved them considerably, but it marked Carl's coming of age. "From the date of this trip," he wrote, "my goals, values, aims, and philosophy have been my own" (Kirschenbaum, 1979, p. 26).

Carl's parents' influence, we may say in summary, was primarily to instill a set of moral values in their son. The importance of leading a meaningful life and devoting oneself to the welfare of others was a central part of Rogers's heritage. So too, however, was a great amount of repression and a judgmental outlook. As he grew into manhood, Carl retained the former values while rejecting the latter. His rebellion was not extreme, but it was clear and unwavering. Once he had found the stance that suited him, he assumed it with conviction. In essence, however, it was merely a modernization of what his parents stood for, a liberalization of what was valuable in their conservatism. Carl, we may say, retained the *spirit* of Christianity—the spirit of faith, hope, charity, and reverence for life—while rejecting its dogmatism.

This kind of departure from the status quo became Rogers's style throughout his professional career. A frequent innovator, he was never a revolutionary. He modernized and humanized psychology and psychotherapy, made the field more reasonable, more accepting and benign, but never lost the moral fervor that was ingrained in him as a youth. As was said of Aristotle, he was an extremist in defense of moderation, and this distinctive blend of characteristics derived directly from his solution to the conflicts in his upbringing.

Meanwhile, however, another important element of Carl's life was taking shape. Before embarking on the China trip, he had fallen in love with Helen Elliott, a girl he had known since childhood. They had started to see each other constantly and while away he wrote her regularly. When he returned, the romance grew. As he confided to his journal, "There have been times when we have been together . . . when it has seemed to both of us that we have loved each other with an intensity that simply couldn't be measured—when mind and soul and body are just flooded in a mighty tide of love. And then there are times when we have opened the secret chambers of our personalities to each other and, oh, the treasures I've found hidden in those inner sanctuaries!" (Kirschenbaum, 1979, p. 37). They were married in 1924 and promptly moved to New York, where Carl attended Union Theological Seminary.

He had chosen this institution largely because of its liberal orientation and he was not disappointed in the training he received. One event, in particular, impressed him greatly. "A group of students, of which I was one, felt that ideas were being fed to us and that we were not having an opportunity to discuss the religious and philosophical issues which most deeply concerned us. We wanted to explore our own questions and doubts and find out where they led. We petitioned the administration that we be allowed to set up a seminar (for credit!) in which there would be no instructor and in which the curriculum would be composed of our own questions. The Seminary was understandably perplexed by this request but they granted our petition. . . . This seminar was deeply satisfying and clarifying. It moved me a long way toward a philosophy of life which was my own. The majority of the members of that group, in thinking their way through the questions they had raised, thought their way right out of religious work. I was one" (Kirschenbaum, 1979, p. 51).

While attending UTS, Carl had taken several courses in psychology and progressive education at Teachers College, Columbia. In 1926, he left UTS and enrolled at Columbia to earn his doctorate in educational and clinical psychology. In the same year, Helen gave birth to their first child, David, and Carl underwent a successful operation on a duodenal ulcer. Called "the intellectual's ulcer" by some, this event may have been a harbinger of trouble to come, or at least indicative of a great deal of repressed emotion in the fledgling psychologist.

In 1928, the Rogers's moved to Rochester, where they lived until 1939. Carl worked at the Society for the Prevention of Cruelty to Children, doing counseling, testing, and lecturing. His faith in human nature was already clearly apparent. "Most children," he wrote at the time, "if given a reasonably normal environment which meets their own emotional, intellectual, and social needs, have within themselves sufficient drive toward health to respond and make a comfortable adjustment to life" (Kirschenbaum, 1979, p. 35)—a statement heralding the viewpoint that would distinguish his professional career.

Unimpressed with psychoanalysis, which he found impractical, too uninterested in the patient's present environment, and apt to exaggerate ordinary problems that everybody shares, Carl also contested the dominance of psychiatry in the practice of psychotherapy. Psychologists, he argued, could do as effective counseling as psychiatrists, besides which they were not hampered by the medical tendency to look upon patients as "sick."

In his thirties, he became familiar with the work of Otto Rank and his students, Jessie Taft and Frederick Allen. Rank believed that all people are caught in a conflict between their "will-to-health" and their "will-to-illness." The aim of therapy, he taught, should be to help the individual accept himself and free his will-to-health. Rogers found this point of view congenial and enjoyed his association with the Rankians. As he told me in our interview, however, "I never had a mentor . . . I think that, to an unusual degree, my work was born out of direct experience."

In 1939, Carl wrote his first major book, *The Clinical Treatment of the Problem Child*. Shortly thereafter, he accepted a professorship at Ohio State and the family moved to Columbus. By this time the Rogers's had had their second child, Natalie. Both children, when interviewed as adults, remembered their father as a calm, firm, reasonable, honest, and meticulous man. Strong negative feelings were not allowed to disturb their home, however. If you were angry, you were expected to go to your room and cool off.

Helen assumed the responsibilities of homemaking, giving Carl the mobility to advance in his profession. Like so many women of her generation, she appears to have done it willingly, but many years later to have felt some resentment at the domestic role to which she had been relegated.

Throughout their long marriage—Helen died in 1979—Carl and Helen's relationship was very close. They also maintained close ties with their children, both of whom continued to confide in their parents and relate to them in a very open way long after they had married and had children of their own. In contrast to some psychologists, Carl practiced what he preached. His personal life is a testament to the integrity of his behavior and beliefs.

In the last years of Helen's life, however, when she was becoming increasingly bedridden, Carl felt impelled to continue his independent activities instead of spending the bulk of his time nursing his wife. This decision caused him a good deal of soul-searching. As he wrote in 1980, "In these last years the distance between us had grown increasingly great. I wanted to care for her, but I was not at all sure that I loved her. One day, when she was very near death, I was in an internal frenzy which I could not understand at all. When I went to the hospital as usual to feed her her supper, I found myself pouring out to her how much I had loved her, how much she had meant in my life, how many positive initiatives she had contributed to our long partnership" (*A Way of Being,* 1980, p. 91).

The transparency with which he reveals himself here is more characteristic of Rogers than of any other leading psychologist. In passage after passage of his writings, he tells us exactly what he did and felt, with no inclination to justify himself, castigate himself, or make more of himself than is readily apparent. Here I am, he seems to say in the simplest possible way. No posturing, no pretentiousness, no long-winded diatribes or involved explanations. As a result, he sometimes seems bland or ingenuous— never, however, dishonest or defensive.

*Counseling and Psychotherapy,* Rogers's second major work and the book that established his reputation, was published in 1942. Here, for the first time in print, he used the term "client" instead of "patient." While it may seem a minor matter, the change of this single word betokened a major shift in the model of what the relationship between a psychotherapist and one who seeks help should be. In place of the imperious doctor-as-healer and patient-as-invalid notion that had so far prevailed in the field, Rogers was proposing the idea of an alliance, a consultative interaction between the therapist, who possesses certain skills and knowledge, and the client, who has the solutions to his problems within, but needs to recognize them and allow them to function fully. Such a shift was already implicit in psychoanalysis, particularly of the Jungian variety; but Rogers solidified the transformation by making it fully explicit.

As Kirschenbaum says, "With each chapter of *Counseling and Psychotherapy,* the system in Rogers's therapy emerged with cumulative clarity. With all his ambivalences, the client wants to grow, wants to mature, wants to face his problems and work them through. Accept and clarify his initial expressions of feeling, and a fuller, deeper expression of feelings will follow. Accept and clarify these and insight will spontaneously occur. Accept and clarify these insights, and the client will begin to take positive actions in his life, based on his insight. Accept and clarify the meaning the client sees in his positive actions, and at some point, when he feels enough self-acceptance, self-understanding, and confidence in his ability to continue to deal with his own problems, he will end the relationship" (Kirschenbaum, 1979, p. 128).

Rogers's approach to therapy, as we can see from this passage, was simple and systematic. Systematic simplicity, in fact, is a hallmark of his style, as it is a distinguishing feature of the man. In his writing, teaching, counseling, as well as in private conversation, he is careful and thoughtful, sticking with a point until he has made it clear, while the qualities of disputatiousness and flooding of ideas that color the works of other leaders of the field are notably absent.

Elaborating on what I said earlier about Carl's "coming of age," let me also observe that his divergence from the psychiatric doctrine of the day was not unlike his divergence from his parents' fundamentalist beliefs. What he did, in both cases, was take a stand opposed to the authoritarianism and complacency of those in power, staking his faith on the ability of the average person to find his own salvation and casting himself as an ally to that multitude of seekers.

The Rogerian system of therapy had actually been proposed a couple of years earlier. Carl had been invited to deliver a speech at the University of Minnesota. The date was Dec. 11, 1940. In his address, he had spelled out the principles of his brand of treatment—e.g., "The aim of this newer therapy is not to solve one particular problem, but to assist the individual to grow, so that he can cope with the present problem and with later problems in a better integrated fashion"—and was astounded at the furor he stirred up. As he said in our interview, "The first time I became aware that I was saying something different was at a talk I gave at the University of Minnesota. I thought everyone had agreed with me and I thought everything was moving in that direction. Then I was shocked and horrified when the big reaction set in, so then I began to realize that I was working along new lines. . . . The fact that it would gradually develop into something larger and larger was not even considered. At that time my thoughts and ideas had no implications outside of therapy."

In any case, with the publication of *Counseling and Psychotherapy*, Rogers became a significant innovator in the treatment of people with psychological problems. The book was at first ignored by the psychological establishment, but its popularity grew steadily with students and younger psychologists, and Carl's subsequent lectures and publications made it increasingly clear that he had something important to say.

He moved to the University of Chicago in 1945, and the next 12 years turned out to be the most productive period of his life. He published three books and close to 60 articles, became an officer of many prestigious groups, won numerous awards and honors, was elected president of the American Psychological Association, and acquired immense prestige.

On what, we may ask, was his rise to eminence founded? As the originator of a new approach to therapy, he was not alone. There were other innovators in the field, and what Rogers stood for was not that radical. The therapist as an accepting, nonjudgmental listener, one who refrains from giving advice, and one who has faith in the clients' ability to find their own solutions—these precepts were not unknown, although Rogers applied them more systematically than anyone had previously done.

The Rogerian approach, however, was both congruent with trends in American life—in particular, the trend toward permissiveness and antiauthoritarianism—and with one of the primary values of American psychology, its increasing respect for operationism and scientific research. Carl published verbatim records of himself doing therapy, thereby rescuing the procedure from the realms of speculation and making it available for all to examine. Further, he committed himself to conducting research on the effectiveness of his approach, publishing his findings in respected journals and making no attempt to glorify the results.

Here then was a man for our time: a homegrown American psychologist, full professor at a leading university, acknowledging the importance of the scientific method, while forging a brand of treatment free of such questionable concepts as the Jungian archetypes or the Freudian Oedipus complex. On top of that, Carl's personal qualities—his mild-mannered, pleasant determination, his eloquence in writing, his tenacity in pursuing the goals in which he believed, his reasonableness and thoughtfulness—added up to a formidable force. He has said that he was simply the exponent of ideas whose time had come, but we must not fail to note what an excellent exponent he was.

Despite his achievements, however, the road Carl was yet to take was by no means without its pitfalls. To begin with the most surprising, during the years 1949 to 1951 he experienced such personal distress that he came close to a serious mental breakdown. The most apparent outer cause was a difficult client whom Rogers had taken on for treatment. Instead of improving, however, or choosing to end the relationship, she became more and more dependent on him, and more and more demanding.

In his own words: "There was a deeply disturbed client with whom I had worked fairly extensively at Ohio State, who later moved to the Chicago area and renewed her therapeutic contacts with me. . . . She began to take up a bigger and bigger part of my therapy time—two or three times a week. She would sometimes appear sitting on our doorstep. I felt trapped by this kind of dependence. She said she needed more warmth and more realness from me. I wanted her to like me though I didn't like her. This brought about the most intense hostility on her part (along with dependence and love), which completely pierced my defenses I recognized that many of her insights were sounder than mine, and this destroyed my confidence in myself . . . I literally lost the boundaries of myself. . . . The efforts of colleagues to help were of no avail, and I became convinced (and I think with some reason) that I was going insane" (Kirschenbaum, 1979, pp. 191–2).

His reaction appears extreme, so we may speculate that there was more going on in Rogers's life, or more to his feelings about this woman, than he was able to articulate. Approaching fifty, he had already served as president of the APA and achieved distinguished status. Yet here was a client he could not help—an understandable blow to his pride, but many another professional has withstood occasional failure with greater equanimity. Why then did he slip to the edge? Did the client's demands for more warmth and genuineness expose his Achilles's heel? Did her psychosis (for she was a borderline psychotic) seem to repudiate his faith in people's inherent health, or were there other issues undermining his composure?

Commenting on the episode at a later date, Rogers said it made him feel "rather deeply certain of my complete inadequacy as a therapist, my worthlessness as a person, and my lack of any future in the field of psychology or psychotherapy" (Kirschenbaum, 1979, p. 193). At the very least, then, his frustration over this client exposed a deep strain of self-doubt one might never have suspected in this highly successful man.

Nor was his way of coping with the dilemma anything of which to be proud. Without warning the client in advance, Rogers asked a psychiatrist friend to take over the case. During the very next interview, according to their prearranged plan, the psychiatrist entered the office unannounced, Rogers introduced him and simply walked out. Thereupon the client regressed into a full-blown psychotic state. Carl hurried home, told his wife they had to get away, and within an hour they were on the road on a "runaway trip" that lasted several months.

It is to his credit, I think, that on his return Rogers went into therapy to come to terms with the feelings of shame and bewilderment aroused in him by this fiasco, and even more to his credit that he later allowed an account of it to be published, with no attempt to alibi his behavior at the time.

By now Rogers's method of treatment had established itself as a major contribution to the field. It was not to remain static, however. From the mid-1950s on, Carl began to use the term "congruence" with increasing frequency when describing his work. "It appears essential that the therapist be genuine, or whole, or congruent in the relationship. What this means is that it is important for the therapist to be what he is in his contact with the client. To the extent that he presents an outward facade of one attitude or feeling, while inwardly or at an unconscious level he experiences another feeling, the likelihood of successful therapy will be diminished" (Kirschenbaum, 1979, p. 196).

Later, in the 1960s, he became involved with the human potential movement that was flourishing in California, and adopted some of their credos. The importance of frank and immediate expression of feeling, the healing power of physical intimacy, the belief in each individual's responsibility for his own destiny, the value of conducting—or "facilitating," as Rogers prefers to say—large groups in place of the more traditional one-to-one treatment setting: all became parts of the evolving Rogerian method.

In 1957, Carl moved to the University of Wisconsin. He remained there until 1963, but later called those 6 years "the most painful and anguished episode in my whole professional life." What apparently happened was this. Using half a million dollars in funding that he had obtained from various grants, Rogers and three colleagues—Eugene Gendlin, Charles Truax, and Donald

Kiesler—set up a research project on the treatment of schizophrenics and normals through the therapeutic relationship. There were 48 subjects in all: 16 acute schizophrenics, 16 chronic schizophrenics, and 16 normal volunteers. Each group was divided into 8 matched pairs and, by a flip of a coin, one of each pair was given therapy. Eight therapists, Rogers being one, saw 3 patients each. The clients took a battery of tests and were interviewed by an independent judge every 3 months. Every single interview was recorded and transcribed, and the task of analyzing the data and writing up the findings was divided between the four colleagues and their assistants.

The book that resulted, however—*The Therapeutic Relationship and Its Impact: A Study of Psychotherapy with Schizophrenics*—appeared only in 1967, for the years between were filled with acrimonious dissension between the authors. In the process of analyzing their data, they began to distrust each other, and eventually to criticize Rogers for failing to take a strong leadership role. Truax's data mysteriously disappeared and were never recovered, lawsuits were threatened, and in the end the study found "no significant differences between the therapy group and the control group as to process movement in therapy and only some small differences as to outcomes of therapy." For the most part, however, "high therapist conditions of congruence and empathy did correlate with successful outcomes of therapy" (Kirschenbaum, 1979, pp. 287–8).

Carl and Helen moved to La Jolla in 1964. He began to spend more time on his hobbies—gardening, photography, and building mobiles—but continued to write and lecture widely. *On Becoming a Person*, his most popular book, had appeared in 1961. *Freedom to Learn: A View of What Education Might Become,* was to be published in 1969, *Carl Rogers on Encounter Groups* in 1970, *Becoming Partners: Marriage and its Alternatives* in 1972, *Carl Rogers: The Man and His Ideas* in 1975, *Carl Rogers on Personal Power* in 1977, and *A Way of Being* in 1980. That is not to speak of the many articles and chapters he continued to contribute to various journals and texts. In 1956, he had received the Distinguished Scientific Contribution Award from the APA, and in 1972 he was to receive the Distinguished Professional Contribution Award from the same organization. Yet in the years 1968–1969 he again experienced "events which have given me more agony than anything else I can recall in my professional life."

With other colleagues, he had formed a group called Western Behavioral Sciences Institute. The collaboration of the members worked well for the first few years, but their cohesiveness gradually deteriorated into warring factions. Carl was unable or unwilling to wield power to unite them, so he eventually resigned and formed a new group called the Center for Studies of the Person.

This repeated experience of dismay over the inability of people with whom he associated himself to get along with each other calls for speculation on our part. According to some of his closest associates, the situation stemmed from Rogers's refusal to take command. Believing as strongly as he always did in the ability of people to solve their own problems, Carl consistently declined to issue orders or use strong persuasive measures, even when these might have brought the groups of which he was a member into line.

On a deeper level, it has been suggested that a fundamental flaw in Rogers's view of human nature can be seen in his experience with his contentious colleagues—as well, it should be added, as with the client who caused him his near-breakdown in 1951, and in the disappointing results of the schizophrenic treatment project at the University of Wisconsin. What all these events add up to, it has been argued, is a refutation of Carl's rosy outlook on life. As Kirschenbaum puts it, Rogers maintained that "at his core, the human being is basically socialized, constructive, and trustworthy. . . . It has been said that this opinion of human nature is unsound for those whose profound conflicts show the deeper, darker, demonic side of human nature" (p. 286).

In our first interview, I asked him about this matter. His reply was that, while he had been gravely disappointed a couple of times by putting more trust in people than was warranted, in the vast majority of his interactions he felt that his trust was justified. In fact, he suggested, it is like a self-fulfilling prophecy. If you invest your trust in people, they are likely to live up to it; if you approach them with distrust, they will be inclined to live up to that.

However that may be, Rogers's latter years were apparently free of dissension. Since Helen's death, he told me, he had had relationships with other women, but he lived alone in his comfortable home overlooking La Jolla bay. His involvement in the human potential movement brought about a change in his manner of relating to others. He became more demonstrative in showing his feelings and he clearly had no trouble forming close and meaningful liaisons. He maintained a warm contact with his children and grandchildren, made occasional public appearances, did a good deal of writing, and enjoyed the admiration of a vast and growing public.

One of his main professional interests in the last 10 years of his life was to spark a reassessment of our educational procedures. In *Freedom to Learn,* (1969) he said, "We possess a very considerable knowledge of the conditions which encourage self-initiated, significant, experiential, 'gut-level' learning by the whole person. . . . The initiation of such learning rests not upon the teaching skills of the leader, not upon his scholarly knowledge of the field, not upon his curricular planning, not upon his use of audiovisual aids, not upon the programmed learning he utilizes, not upon his lectures and presentations, not upon an abundance of books. . . . No, the facilitation of significant learning rests upon certain attitudinal qualities which exist in the personal *relationship* between the facilitator and the learner" (pp. 105–6).

This notion, that teachers should be facilitators of learning rather than conveyors of information or judges of excellence, was not kindly received by the educational establishment. Here as elsewhere, Rogers was accused of superficiality and overoptimism; but *Freedom to Learn* has sold close to half a million copies and many students, if not their instructors, find it highly inspiring.

Another dominant interest I learned about when I visited him for a second time in 1986 was his active participation in attempts to ameliorate interracial and international tensions. He had facilitated groups in South Africa, Brazil, Austria, Hungary, and the USSR, and was enthusiastic as well as deeply moved by the responses he had witnessed.

The fight he waged in these arenas show that Carl in his eighties was anything but placid. Neither detached nor disillusioned, he took a lively interest in the human enterprise and continued to contribute his particular ray of light to our common quest for enlightenment to the very end.

Summing up their views of his character and achievements, his colleagues have made some perceptive observations. *Howard Kirschenbaum* (1979): "People often picture Carl Rogers as a totally accepting, warm, and understanding person. While these characteristics certainly do describe him, they definitely do not comprise his entire repertoire of responses. Whenever Rogers's personal or professional interests have been threatened, he has been extremely tenacious about getting his own way" (p. 103).

*Norman Brice*: "Someone, somewhere who does understand Carl said of him that he has a 'whim of steel.' Carl is nobody's pushover. He is a very, very strong and controversial man" (Kirschenbaum, 1979, p. 186).

*T. M. Tomlinson*: "Rogers doesn't give love; he is fairly lovable but not very loving. That, I think, is what leads to the conclusion that he's cold, i.e., people approach him expecting to be loved immediately for what they are, whereas Carl simply accepts them for what they are without implications of love" (Kirschenbaum, 1979, p. 189).

*Rosalind Dymond Cartwright*: "Carl provided a role model for a couple of generations of therapists, clinical psychologists, counseling people and others. . . . He is a man who has continued to grow, to discover himself, to test himself, to be genuine, to review his experience, to learn from it, and to fight the good fight, which means to stand up and be counted, to stand for something, to live honestly, fully, in the best human sense" (Kirschenbaum, 1979, p. 394).

*Richard Farson:* "Perhaps more than anyone, he made psychology the business of normal people and normal people the business of psychology . . . He successfully challenged the medical model . . . (but) by and large, he is unable to recognize the coexistence of opposites or the enormous complexity of human affairs. . . . Rogers would have you believe that the more congruence, the more honesty, the more intimacy, the more closeness, the more empathy, the better. Sounds good, but . . . it fails in the extreme, and that unfortunately is where it is taken by both Rogers and his students" (Evans, 1985 introduction).

And finally, *Bruce Meador:* "Carl is a passionate person. . . . There is nothing flamboyant about his appearance or life-style. He does not raise his voice above a clear conversational level.

He is not colorful. . . . The only thing he really flirts with is being stuffy, but he doesn't make it. His passion shines through" (Kirschenbaum, 1979, p. 399).

As I had the opportunity, I asked Rogers how he felt about two matters I had not found explicated in his writings. First, the many followers he has acquired over the years, the people who call themselves "Rogerians." "I really feel sorry for them sometimes," he said. "I try very hard not to develop disciples, but I can't control them. Some people become disciples. People who work with me whom I value most (however) are those who went their own way, developed their own lines of thinking."

Second, I asked about his sense of humor. "I think in two ways I have a sense of humor," he replied. "One you might not call humor. I think one of the things I treasure about myself is in one sense I take my work very seriously and in another sense I take it very lightly. I am only one speck in this enormous universe, so I struggle along here to do what I can, and that is an amazing thing to think we are something important. Then the other kind of humor is, my humor is a sort of wry, light humor, turning a serious conversation into something funny with a pun, or with some other turn of phrase. I am not a joke teller, I almost never tell jokes."

It is interesting to note in this context that Carl has been the target of spoofing by both his colleagues and his students. A joke that has been repeated ad nauseum has him counseling a suicidal client. "I wish I was dead," says the client. "You feel so bad you don't even want to live," reflects Rogers. "Yes, I want to kill myself." "You'd actually like to end it all." "As a matter of fact, I'm going to jump out of this tenth story window." "Your intention is to commit suicide by leaping out of my office window." "That's right," says the client, as he jumps. Whereupon Rogers gets up, looks out, and says, "Plop!"[1]

It seems to me that Carl in his prime was a good butt for wit precisely because of his style and his image. His undeviatingly nondirective method seemed so unnatural to many people that it lent itself to caricature. One has only to take it a step or two farther to make it ridiculous. At the same time, Rogers appeared to be such a decent and virtuous person that he invited derision if only to make him more human.

Happily, as I found in our interviews, he was not unable to see himself in humorous perspective. Nor was he without wit or playfulness. As he described it, however, his humor was hardly robust. Its primary attribute was probably "philosophical," and that, I believe, is a clue to his character—fine, intellectual, moral, but a little straitlaced. The impression I had in our meetings was of a genuine, thoughtful, and modest man, centered in himself yet not in the least overbearing. His demeanor, I now think, was somewhat misleading, at least to the extent that it failed to convey the unflagging industry with which he pursued his goals. (On reading an early draft of this account, Rogers wrote me that while "for the most part it seems very accurate . . . I am glad I am not really as serious-minded as you make me out to be." At our second meeting I saw that he had a point, for he not only gave examples of how he occasionally engaged in mild banter with his clients but also laughed delightedly when I became bold enough to "kid" him personally.)

Nevertheless, Carl Rogers the man was no enigma. His characteristics were fully evident in his writings, his career, and his public self. If the observations put forth by his colleagues and myself are accepted, two questions remain to be answered. How did he become the kind of person he was? And what was the relationship between his character structure and his therapeutic method?

The facts we have surveyed suggest that Rogers was both a product of his upbringing and a liberalization of its values. In an essay entitled, "This is Me" (*On Becoming a Person*, 1961, pp. 3–27), he stressed the closeness of his family, their high moral standards, and their "worship of the virtue of hard work." He clearly carried this Puritan ethic into his own life. Later he told about his father's determination to operate his farm on a scientific basis and said that his own respect for science had its roots in this part of his early experience. As a young man, however, Carl abandoned his mother's righteousness, her tendency to look down on other people's moral failings, and his parents' rigid fundamentalism, replacing them with a faith in humanity and the increasingly firm belief that, if he could give people "unconditional positive regard," they would grow toward the valuable goals of self-acceptance and self-actualization. (He himself had received such regard at Union Theological Seminary, and the permissive environment of that institution had enabled him to find his true vocation.) In this crucial step he began to affirm his self-worth and become the individual the world would eventually acclaim.

It should be emphasized that Rogers's nonjudgmental attitude was more than an act of grace. He appears to have been driven into it by an intense need to separate from his mother and overcome her restrictive influence. To some extent, in fact, his entire therapeutic style—the accepting, trusting, nondirective approach the world now knows as "Rogerian"—was what Jung would have called a compensation for the directive, judgmental atmosphere in which he was raised. Nevertheless, the fact remains that he made an art of his need and transformed it into a potent instrument of therapeutic change.

Having found a set of values that felt right to him, Carl was indefatigable in establishing them in psychology. His work became a vehicle for his personal development, his findings and theories an extension of his essential self. Hard work, clear thinking, uprightness of character, a happy combination of clinical and scientific ability, and eloquence in prose led him into a position of leadership in the field. Because he was intent on independent thought, no less than because he believed in each person's ability to find his own solutions, he could not give his allegiance to psychoanalysis or behaviorism. Because he had faith in free will and knew, from his own experience, that one could break away from the past and live an authentic life based on present decisions and inner direction, he was destined to become a humanist before that position had been fully estabished in the field. His psychological stance, in other words, was both an outgrowth of his person and an affirmation of his liberalized belief system.

Looking at his career in comparison to some of the other great psychologists we have discussed, we may conclude that Rogers did not create an intricate worldview as Freud had done, nor foreshadow a set of countercultural values as Jung had done, nor dismiss the "inner man" as Skinner had done. Neither an empire-builder like Freud, an abstruse philosopher like Jung, nor a visionary mechanist like Skinner, he was part of the "permissiveness and authenticity movement" that reached its apex in the 1960s, became one of its spokespersons, and played a large part in validating it. In contrast to Freud's brilliant shrewdness, Jung's mystical profundity, and Skinner's materialistic ingenuity, Rogers's primary virtues were genuineness without excess, gentle patience, openness to change and, above all, faith in the ordinary human being.

To some, Rogers's merits seem too simple to warrant the honors he received. His detractors have portrayed him as conscientious to a fault and incapable of spontaneity. His ability to express warmth has been impugned and his understanding of human nature has been called superficial. These allegations, I believe, are based on a poor understanding of the man.

In an essay entitled, "What it Means to Become a Person," (*On Becoming a Person*, 1961, pp. 115–123), Rogers defined four characteristics he thought were central to personal growth. They are, first, *openness to experience* (i.e., the ability to take in the evidence of a new situation, to tolerate ambiguity and relinquish defensiveness); second, *trust in one's organism* (i.e., after weighing one's feelings, memories, expectations, and awareness of social demands, and in the admission that one may make mistakes, one has faith in one's judgment); third, *an internal locus of evaluation* (i.e., less and less does one look to others for approval or guidance, more and more does one come to feel that what matters is living according to one's truest self); and fourth, *willingness to be a process* (i.e., dropping fixed goals, welcoming change, and realizing that one's self is more a process than a product).

There can be no doubt, I think, that Carl Rogers, both in his life and in his work—which, we should see by now, are practically interchangeable—exhibited these qualities to an unusual degree. He did, in short, precisely what he spent his life encouraging others to do: discovered his core and lived by that standard as truly as he could.

## MILTON H. ERICKSON AND AUTOHYPNOSIS

In contrast to Rogers, Milton H. Erickson was an intentionally directive therapist. His directiveness may have been *in*direct, but he made no attempt to be *non*directive. He saw his patients as people who needed his guidance and took pride in advising (and at times outwitting and manipulating) them for their own good. More than one lonely patient of his "accidentally" became acquainted with another lonely patient by showing up at a time and place Erickson had specified. Family members were instructed to turn their backs on each other and write down everything the other said that was wrong in order to improve their relationships. And in a typical passage describing his therapeutic maneuvers, he once told the following tale.

"Now, a doctor came to me and said, 'I had intercourse the first time in a bawdy house. The experience disgusted me. So much so that in the 20 years that have gone by I have not had a single erection. I have hired women at all levels and paid them big money and told them, "Make me get an erection." And they've all failed. Now I've found a girl I want to marry. I tried to go to bed with her. She's very kind and solicitous, but I can't get an erection.' I said, 'Let the girl talk to me . . . I told the girl, 'Go to bed with him every night, but be a thoroughly cold woman. Don't permit him to touch your breasts, touch your body in any way at all. Just forbid it. And it's very important you obey these instructions.' I called the doctor in and said, 'I told Mildred that she's to go to bed with you every night. I told her to reject any attempt at kissing, touching of her breasts, her genitals, her body. She's to be totally rejecting of you. and I want that to take place for 3 months. Then you come in and discuss the situation with me.' Early in March he lost control of himself and 'raped' her. Now, Mildred was a very beautiful woman with a beautiful figure. And when he was confronted by the impossibility derived from Mildred, *not from him*, it changed the frame of reference. Mildred was making intercourse impossible; he wasn't. *So he didn't have to hang on to his limp penis. Mildred made it impossible for him*" (Rosen, 1983, p. 157).

An exceptionally astute and ingenious practitioner, Erickson was a benign authority figure but an authority figure nonetheless. The fact that he specialized in *hypnotherapy* was indicative of his approach to treatment. While he maintained that the trance simply opened the patient to his own resources—"The hypnotic state is the subject's own accumulated learnings and memories" (*Collected Papers*, Vol. 1, 1980, p. 113)—his stance was akin to that of an administrator who knows how to motivate his employees to perform their duties efficiently. In other words, Erickson was always in the driver's seat. A subtle controller of all who consulted him, he spoke of himself as having "a steel fist in a velvet glove" (Rossi et al., 1983 p. 49), and clearly relished the ease with which he could get people to do what he thought would be beneficial for them.

Biographical accounts by three of Erickson's colleagues and students—Ernest Rossi, Jay Haley, and Ronald A. Havens—portray him as a self-made genius who survived an incredible array of physiological disabilities and devastating illnesses to become an internationally admired exponent of innovative psychotherapy. Born in 1901 in Aurum, Nevada, a now defunct mining town in which his father was trying to strike it rich, Milton suffered an extreme form of color blindness,[2] was arrhythmic and tone-deaf, had dyslexia, and did not learn to talk until the age of four.

As if these problems were not enough, he contracted one strain of polio at the age of seventeen and another at the age of fifty-one. The first bout left him temporarily paralyzed from the neck down; the second permanently denied him the use of his legs, greatly restricted the use of his right arm, and partially restricted the use of his left arm. Eventually, he was able to use only part of his diaphragm to speak, and in his later years he suffered from chronic pain which he moderated with autohypnosis.

As his biographers make clear, however, one of Erickson's most remarkable traits was his capacity for turning disadvantages into advantages. "He was fond of saying that life's difficulties were merely necessary roughage" (Havens, p. xiii), and his youth, in particular, was filled with episodes demonstrating his ability not just to overcome but to capitalize on the obstacles life had strewn in his path.

Since young Milton did not understand how to use the dictionary to look up a word alphabetically, he searched for each word he wanted to find by starting from "A" and proceeding until he located it. As a result, he literally read the dictionary from front to back many times during elementary school, a feat that earned him the nickname "Dictionary." As a schoolboy, Milton also noticed that his classmates frequently hummed songs they had just heard sung on the radio or in concert performances. As he had no ability to carry a tune himself, he began to pay attention to the breathing patterns of the singers. "After some experimentation he found that when he mimicked the patterns of breathing associated with a particular song, those around him would begin humming or even singing that song and assume it was a tune that had just come to them out of the blue. . . . Eventually he became convinced that breathing patterns could be used to communicate a variety of messages in an unobtrusive and unrecognized fashion, a recognition that he often employed when inducing a hypnotic trance" (Havens, p. 10).

Most impressive, however, were Milton's successful endeavors to overcome the debilitating effects of his first attack of polio. Discussing the event with Ernest Rossi many years later, Erickson began by making the point that an autohypnotic experience had initially played a part in his struggle to survive.

E: As I lay in bed that night, I overheard the three doctors tell my parents in the other room that their boy would be dead in the morning. I felt intense anger that anyone should tell a mother her boy would be dead by morning. My mother then came in with as serene a face as can be. I asked her to arrange the dresser, push it up against the side of the bed at an angle. She did not understand why, she thought I was delirious. My speech was difficult. But at that angle by virtue of the mirror on the dresser I could see through the doorway, through the west window of the other room. I was damned if I would die without seeing one more sunset. If I had any skill in drawing, I could still sketch that sunset.

R: Your anger and wanting to see another sunset was a way you kept yourself alive through that critical day in spite of the doctors' predictions. But why do you call that an autohypnotic experience?

E: I saw that vast sunset covering the whole sky. But I know there was also a tree there outside the window, but I blocked it out.

R: You blocked it out? It was that selective perception that enables you to say you were in an altered state?

E: Yes, I did not do it consciously. I saw all the sunset, but I didn't see the fence and large boulder that were there. I blocked out everything except the sunset. After I saw the sunset, I lost consciousness for three days. When I finally awakened, I asked my father why they had taken out that fence, tree, and boulder. I did not realize I had blotted them out when I fixed my attention so intensely on the sunset . . .

R: Would you say it was the intensity of your inner experience, your spirit and sense of defiance, that kept you alive to see that sunset?

E: Yes, I would. With patients who have a poor outlook, you say, "Well, you should live long enough to do this next month" And they do. (Collected Papers, Vol. 1, 1980 pp. 111–112)

When the fever subsided, however, Milton found himself almost completely paralyzed. He could see and move his eyes, hear the slightest sound, and speak, although with difficulty. From the neck down, however, his body was immobilized. The family—Milton had eight sisters and one brother—now lived on a farm in Wisconsin, and there were no rehabilitation facilities nearby. For all his parents knew, their son might have had to remain without the use of his limbs for the rest of his life.

But his thinking ability was unimpaired. He used it, at first, simply to interpret the sounds around him. By listening closely to how the barn door was closed and how long it took a set of footsteps to reach the house, for instance, he learned to tell who was entering and what mood he or she was in. "Then came that critical day when his family forgot they had left him alone, tied into the rocking chair. . . . The rocking chair was somewhere in the middle of the room with Milton in it, looking longingly at the window, wishing he were closer to it so that he could at least have the pleasure of gazing out at the farm. As he sat there, apparently immobile, wishing and wondering, he suddenly became aware that his chair began to rock slightly. . . . This discovery, which probably would have passed unnoticed by most of us, led the seventeen-year-old lad into a feverish period of self-exploration and discovery. Milton was discovering for himself the basic ideo-motor principle of hypnosis discussed by Bernheim a generation earlier: *exercising the thought or the idea of movement could lead to the actual experience of automatic body movement*" (Rossi et al., 1983 pp. 11–12).

At eighteen, Milton systematically began to recall all his childhood movements to help himself relearn muscle coordination.

He visualized moving his arms, hands, and fingers, his legs, feet, and toes, his upper torso, lower torso, and so on, in as much detail and vividness as he could recapture. He also observed his baby sister learning to walk in order to remind himself of the motions one has to go through to acquire this fundamental skill (see "Learning to Stand Up" later in this chapter).

After a year of intensive self-training, he was on crutches but otherwise beginning to resume a normal routine of living. He entered the University of Wisconsin and, after his freshman year, was advised by a doctor at the health service to spend the summer in nature to strengthen his limbs. He decided to take a canoe trip through the lakes of Madison, down the O'Hare River, the Rock River, the Mississippi, and back up the Illinois. In the course of this adventure he became adept at soliciting aid, without exactly asking for it, to accomplish those tasks he could not handle himself. Portaging the canoe, setting up his tent, even scrounging for food became challenges to his ingenuity in getting people to help him. His cordial friendliness won him invitations to many a camper's meal, as well as interesting encounters with others along the way.

"By the time Milton began the return trip, his muscular capacities had increased to the point where he was able to make headway against the river current, and more importantly, to portage the canoe unaided. By the end of the 10-week trip, his list of accomplishments was even more impressive: he had covered 1200 river miles, relying solely on his own ingenuity and resourcefulness; he had begun the trip with $4 and ended it with $8; he had begun the trip on crutches and ended it with only a slight (though permanent) limp; and finally, he had begun the trip a frail lad in ailing health and had ended it a robust young man with a new sense of confidence, pride, and personal independence" (Rossi et al., pp. 14–15).

Milton's enterprising nature showed itself again when he entered medical school. He had arrived in town with a total stake of $75, so he went around looking for a way to support himself. "I saw a house for rent at $70 per month. I looked it over, saw the landlord, gave him $70, and put up a sign, Rooms For Students. I talked the registrar into delaying the payment of fees. I took in students who were working their way through and were delighted to furnish their own linens at a reduced rent. I talked some secondhand storage companies into letting me store some beds and some furniture for them. So I had the place furnished and the rooms rented out. That essentially paid my way through medical school" (Haley, 1985, p. 152).

Not only was he enterprising, however; he was also remarkably foxy. "When I wanted to be full-time in medical school, there was one serious difficulty—no job. So I went down to the State Board of Control, and beginning in September, every week I had one or two statistical reports on criminality put on the desk of the President of the State Board of Control. They were things he was interested in for getting better appropriations, getting news story releases. Then in November, the first Monday, there was no report. The President was furious, and he demanded that I be called in. He asked me point-blank what I was being paid for. Why didn't I have more reports? I told him I wasn't being paid anything. So he said, 'Well, if that's the case you're on the payroll right now!' " (Haley, 1985, p. 152).

At the age of twenty-three, while still in medical school, Milton married for the first time. This union, which lasted 10 years and produced three children, ended in divorce. Meanwhile, he had completed his B.A. in 1927, his M.A. in psychology, and M.D. in 1928. After completing his residency in psychiatry, he worked at Worcester State Hospital in Massachusetts from 1930 to 1934, then became Director of Psychiatric Research at Wayne County General Hospital in Eloise, Michigan, a post he held until 1948. He married his second wife, Elizabeth, while teaching at Wayne State where she was a psychology student. They had five children in addition to raising Erickson's first three. In 1948, primarily because of his health, they moved to Phoenix, where he established a private practice. The remainder of his life was spent in Phoenix, practicing his unique blend of psychotherapy and hypnotherapy while developing an international reputation and acquiring a host of admirers.

As described by Rossi, Erickson was, in Jungian terminology, an extroverted sensation type. In his old age, he could be crusty and cantankerous, and throughout his life he was notably garrulous. He loved to tell stories to make a point and influence his listeners. He embellished his yarns to suit the occasion, but while their details therefore varied, their essential messages remained the same. In his prime, he had "a burgeoning family of eight children, an ever-growing progression of assorted dogs, and an expanding professional reputation as editor, consultant to such varied groups as the U.S. Rifle Team, to government agencies involved in studying aircraft accidents, and to outstanding athletes who sought to maximize their performance potentials through the use of hypnosis. His lecturing to professional groups expanded across the country . . . he was toasted internationally when he gave hypnotic demonstrations in front of professional groups in many countries where, since he could not speak the languages, he invented the spectacular pantomime techniques of hypnotic induction" (Rossi, 1983, pp. 38–39).

Despite his increasing fame, however, he remained an unpretentious, though utterly confident man. His first office had held only a card table and two chairs, but he discounted the sparseness of the furnishings by explaining, "*I* was there!" In Phoenix, he practiced in his home. As part of the ambience, "Patients constantly tripped over agreeable dogs and children in the family living room that also doubled as a waiting-room, a basset hound named Roger was so relaxed lying in the middle of the floor that patients often fell into reverie and trance just by watching him. . . . Indeed, it wasn't so much a matter of doctor-patient relationships as of family-patient relationships. Children would draw pictures for patients, and little sweet-nothing gifts would be exchanged . . . Since all elements of home, family, and therapy were so marvelously intermixed, it was only natural that Erickson began to use homilies and stories about the family—and particularly about the children's developmental stages of learning—as indirect suggestions to stimulate patients' own healing and growth processes. It was plain to all that this was The Family Man with the steadfast, homespun values of Middle America" (Rossi, 1983, p. 43).

One of the most impressive stories Erickson employed was reprinted by Sidney Rosen (in *My Voice Will Go with You*, Norton, 1982). He called it, "Learning to Stand Up."

> I had a baby sister who had begun to learn to creep. I would have to learn to stand up and walk. And you can imagine the intensity with which I watched as my baby sister grew from creeping

to learning how to stand up. And you don't know how you learned how to stand up. You don't even know how you walked. . . .

You don't know what you do when you walk. You don't know how you learned to stand up. You learned by reaching up your hand and pulling yourself up. That put pressure on your hands—and, by accident, you discovered that you could put weight on your feet. That's an awfully complicated thing because your knees would give way—and, when your knees would keep straight, your hips would give way. Then you got your feet crossed. And you couldn't stand up because both your knees and your hips would give way. Your feet were crossed—and you soon learned to get a wide brace—and you pull yourself up and you have the job of learning how to keep your knees straight—one at a time and as soon as you learn that, you have to learn how to give your attention to keep your hips straight. Then you found out that you had to learn to give your attention to keep your hips straight and knees straight at the same time and feet far apart! Now finally you could stand having your feet far apart, resting on your hands.

Then came the lesson in three stages. You distribute your weight on your one hand and your two feet, this hand not supporting you at all [E. raises his left hand]. Honestly hard work—allowing you to learn to stand up straight, your hips straight, knees straight, feet far apart, this hand (right hand) pressing down hard. Then you discover how to alter your body balance. You alter your body balance by turning your head, turning your body. You have to learn to coordinate all alterations of your body balance when you move your hand, your head, your shoulder, your body—and then you have to learn it all over again with the other hand. Then comes the terribly hard job of learning to have both hands up and moving your hands in all directions and to depend upon the two solid bases of your feet, far apart. And keeping your hips straight—your knees straight and keeping your mind's attention so divided that you can attend to your knees, your hips, your left arm, your right arm, your head, your body. And finally, when you had enough skill, you tried balancing on one foot. That was a hell of a job! (pp. 47–49)

A wonderful example of his observational acumen as well as his dramatic flair for reminding people of their learning power and ability to conquer life's developmental tasks, "Learning to Stand Up" shows Erickson at his subtly encouraging best. In his efforts to help his patients, however, he could also be shockingly provocative.

In another example recorded in *My Voice Will Go With You* ("Vicious Pleasure,"), a woman in her thirties told him that her father had used her as a sex object from the time she was six until she was seventeen. She had put herself through college and earned a B.A. and an M.A. in an attempt to revive her self-respect, but it had not helped. She had become a prostitute, then lived with various men so they would support her, but said she feared sex and found it a painful, horrible experience. "I feel like filth," were her words. "An erect penis just terrifies me and I just get helpless and weak and passive. I am so glad when a man finishes."

Instead of the sympathetic response one would expect at this point, Erickson reportedly replied, "That's an unhappy story; and the really unhappy part is—you're stupid! You tell me that you are afraid of a bold, erect, hard penis—and that's stupid! *You* know you have a vagina; I know it. A vagina can take the biggest, boldest, most assertive penis and turn it into a dangling, helpless object. And your vagina can take a vicious pleasure in reducing it to a helpless, dangling object." Explaining his method to Rosen, he added, "The change on her face was wonderful . . . I called her stupid. I really got her attention. And then I said, '*Vicious* pleasure.' And she did resent men. I also said 'pleasure' " (pp. 36–37).

One more story may serve to suggest the range of Erickson's therapeutic interventions.[3] A student once approached him with concern about a maiden aunt who had made multiple suicide attempts. Instead of attempting to arrange an appointment at his office, Erickson simply showed up at the woman's home the next day where she lived alone with her maid. When she came to the door, he introduced himself and asked to be given a tour of the house. Surprised but intrigued, she agreed to show him around.

In the sun porch, he noticed a row of pots containing African violets. The lady informed him that one thing she had a touch for was growing these plants. He also learned that she went to church every Sunday, but other than that had no meaningful social life. Upon leaving, therefore, he said to her, "Madame, here is your prescription. I want you to send your maid to the nursery to purchase many more pots and every strain of African violet they carry. Furthermore, whenever a child is born to a member of your congregation, I want you to give a pot of African violets to the parents at the baptism. And whenever a wedding is celebrated, I want you to give a pot of these flowers to the bride."

Twenty years later, he recalled, he clipped an article from the local newspaper. "THE AFRICAN VIOLET QUEEN DIES AT AGE 76 . . . " it began, and went on to recount a touching tale of how appreciated this woman had been in her church and community. In telling this story to a group of therapists shortly before his death, Erickson concluded with the remark, "I never did know what was wrong with that woman"—a disingenuous statement, perhaps, but one that underscored his emphasis on results rather than explanations.

Like most outstanding therapists of any orientation, Erickson used his techniques successfully on himself as well. Until he died in 1980, he lived with unceasing illness and pain. To ameliorate his suffering, however, he frequently resorted to autohypnosis. Slipping into a trance was easy for him, and he spent many hours in reverie, reliving the pleasurable moments of his life as a way of diverting his attention from his physical discomfort.

Another technique he used might be called, "Taking charge of one's pain." As he explained it to Rossi, "I may awaken with pain, and I've got to reorient my frame of reference to a state of relaxation, a state of comfort, a state of well-being, into which I am able to drift off into comfortable sleep. It may last the rest of the night. Sometimes it may last no longer than 2 hours, so I'm awakened and must reorient to comfort. Recently the only way I could get control over the pain was by sitting in bed pulling a chair close, and pressing my larynx against the back of the chair. That was very uncomfortable. *But it was discomfort I was deliberately creating*" (Rossi, 1983 pp. 31–32, italics mine).

The implications of this approach go beyond the specifics of dealing with purely physical pain. When any of us, in our attempts to recuperate from relationships or events that have caused us emotional distress, become involved in similar relationships and events, it may not be because we are masochistic or incapable of learning from experience. On the contrary, our choices may represent unwitting attempts at mastery, creating opportunities to "play the game again," this time in the hope that we can take charge of a difficult situation rather than being victimized by it.

Taking charge was a central theme of Erickson's therapeutic system. He took charge of his patients' problems, though only in order to teach them to take charge of themselves. Not only was this a central theme of his work, however; it was a central theme of his life. Erickson's character structure, it should be clear, was composed in large part of the traits of self-reliance, assertiveness, shrewdness, practicality, and strength of will. In no sense was he a shy or retiring individual. Nor was he a theoretician, metaphysician, or intellectual in the academic sense of the word. According to those who knew him best, he was averse to religious beliefs and had no patience with spiritualists, mediums, and other dabblers in the occult. An American original born and bred of pioneer stock, he had all the qualities of those hardy souls who braved the frontier, worked the land, and built themselves homesteads from the raw materials at hand. Canny, sagacious, and enterprising, he was a wily observer of human nature who—happily for those who consulted him—turned his talents to helping others rather than to outfoxing them for gain.

It should not, however, be imagined that Erickson the man had no detractors, or that Erickson the doctor had no therapeutic failures. On the contrary, there were patients who walked out in a huff, objecting to tactics they found invasive and manipulative. There were also professional colleagues who found him objectionably abrasive. His critics, however, were far outnumbered by his admirers. To them he was a genius making significant contributions to the field of mental healing.

Carl Rogers knew Erickson slightly when they were both young men attending the university of Wisconsin. With typical candor, Rogers told me he was embarrassed to recall that at the time he had shied away from Milton because of his physical handicaps. Much later in life, when both were established leaders, Rogers became interested in comparing their approaches to psychotherapy. While Erickson's style was notably at variance with his, he felt they shared many values. Both saw human nature as essentially positive, constructive, and resourceful; both recognized the self-actualizing potential of human beings; both believed in the importance of sensitive understanding on the part of the therapist; both believed in reacting intuitively to their clients' or patients' distress; both placed great emphasis on the uniqueness of the individual; and both had a vision of therapy as a process facilitating reorganization of the self in the directions of becoming "less anxious, guilty, driven, hostile, dependent . . . more secure, self-confident, and aware of experiences previously denied to awareness" (Rogers, 1986).

To return to Erickson himself, however, most important of all was the fact that he was the conqueror of his own infirmities. He endured a lifetime of far greater physical disability than any other mental health leader, but taught himself to make his suffering secondary to his work and enjoyment of living. Beyond that, he learned to use his very disabilities as means to achieve his goals. As Rossi has said, he was the archetype of "the wounded healer," the individual who utilizes his own painful tragedies and what he has learned from them to help his patients work out their own cures.

An ultimate realist who took the raw materials of his endowment, unpromising as they were, and turned them into a highly successful mode of therapy, Erickson was more pragmatic, more insistent on the individuality of his patients, and much more comfortable with "tricking" them for their own good than most other figures in the field. He was also more insistent that "experience is the only teacher"—that patients learn from having or recalling therapeutic experiences, not from principles, theories, or interpretations provided by their therapists.

In compensating for his own perceptual disabilities, he had learned to pay close attention to body language, breathing patterns, and other little-recognized signs of what a person was feeling and thinking, and he used these observations to great advantage as a therapist. He had found, too, that each person's language system is unique, so he urged his disciples to learn what their patients meant by the words they used and as far as possible to speak to them in their own language. He himself tried in scores of ways to help his patients become more objective about their problems and use their experientially acquired skills to solve them. Therapy, in his view, was a learning—or relearning—experience, and while he was unquestionably the teacher, his overriding aim was to instruct others to rely on themselves as successfully as he had done ever since he set out on that canoe trip down the O'Hare.

At the beginning of this chapter, I said, "The more a therapist practices his vocation as an art form, the more likely it becomes that style and techniques of treatment will be colored by personal experience—or to put it more succinctly, the characteristic ways in which such therapists attempt to help others spring directly from whatever helped *them* weather difficult times in their own lives."

Both Rogers's and Erickson's styles and techniques clearly support my thesis. Rogers's nondirectiveness and nonjudgmentalness, his positive regard for others, emphasis on congruence and faith in the client's ability to move in the direction of authenticity and self-acceptance were as much an outgrowth of his ways of finding and affirming himself as Erickson's shrewdness, resourcefulness, and ingenuity in getting his patients to discover their forgotten capacities for adaptation were an outgrowth of *his*.

In this respect, Rogers, Erickson, and all other innovators in the field are little different than poets, painters, or novelists. According to Virginia Woolf, "Every secret of a writer's soul, experience of his life, every quality of his mind is written large in his works." True artists, in other words, create their works out of the raw materials of their personal experience and their creations bear the impress of their conflicts and character traits. In the case of psychotherapists, their creations are simply the styles in which they render their services—more analogous, perhaps, to the distinctive playing styles of musical virtuosos than to the accomplishments of artists who create concrete objects.

In any event, the practice of psychotherapy as an art form seems a peculiarly meaningful undertaking. It is meaningful, on much more than a services-rendered level, to both the practitioner and the receiver, for it constitutes an interaction in which one person, operating out of the depths of his being, attempts to reach, receive, and help transform the depths of another person's being. This dimension makes psychotherapy much more than a technical trade. It makes it a vehicle of ongoing self-exploration for the therapist, since those who practice the profession as an art do not merely bring to it their most intimate characteristics and most deeply held beliefs, but also use it as an opportunity for continued self-definition.

The words of J. Middleton Murry—"An artist, great or small, works for the salvation of his own soul above all other things"— can be be applied to such therapists as readily as to other creative individuals.

1. Another, less widespread, story has Rogers counseling a man who

has great difficulty speaking. They sit thrugh the first interview in silence, since the client cannot talk and Rogers refuses to direct him in any way. At the end of the hour, Rogers collects his fee and the man leaves. The second and third interviews follow the identical pattern. Each time, the participants exchange not a word, the counselor collects his fee, and the client departs. Finally, in the fourth session, the client manages to eke out this phrase. "Dr. Rogers, there's something I want to ask you." "You feel that you want to ask me a question," Rogers replies. "Yes," the client's tortured voice is hopeful. "Tell me please—can you use a partner?" Rogers resents this story, he told me, because he has never engaged in private practice or collected fees for counseling.

2. Because of this condition, purple was the only color he could clearly distinguish. In adulthood, as a result, he took to wearing purple clothing exclusively—a seeming eccentricity actually based on affirming his physiological deficit.

3. This anecdote was related to me by Dr. Norman Berg, who heard it from Erickson in a training session he conducted in the last weeks of his life.

# 7

# A Case In Point[1]

### The Case of Alice W.

I shall call her Alice W. She was twenty years old when she first consulted me in 196–. Her face was pale, framed by long chestnut hair, with a short straight nose, thin lips, and immense dark brown eyes. Searching eyes, soulful eyes, liquid eyes, pooling easily with tears, less easily acquiring a slightly mischievous sparkle, a hint of amusement within their pain. Her voice, throaty, trembled as she spoke, and she sometimes groped for words.

She had been referred by a friend, Alice told me, because she was spending a lot of time crying and had been thinking of dropping out of college. She was in her third year at UCLA. Previously a straight "A" student, she was now either taking incompletes or failing every course in which she was enrolled. It all seemed meaningless to her, going to college, hanging out with other students, drinking, smoking pot, pretending to like rowdy parties and football rallies, but really feeling detached from everyone and everything, often seeing herself as a participant in an empty, foolish charade.

When I inquired about her background, Alice told me she

had been born in Phoenix in 194–. She was an only child and her family had moved to Los Angeles when she was two years old. Her parents, who had never gotten along, had divorced when she was seven or eight. She had remained with her mother. Both mother and father had subsequently remarried, but her contact with her father had always been sporadic. He sent child-support payments and occasionally gave Alice small gifts, but otherwise seemed disinterested in her existence. She portrayed her mother as cold and critical, physically beautiful but entirely self-absorbed. Her father had told her that the reason he had married her mother was that she had informed him (falsely, it turned out) that she was pregnant. He had never loved her, but had felt it was his duty to marry her. Alice believed that she had been conceived in a futile attempt to keep the marriage intact.

Alice's father was a machinist by trade, a hardworking, skillful man who made a comfortable living. He was a kind person, she thought, but taciturn and difficult to contact on a personal level. After her parents had divorced, her mother had married an army officer whom Alice found stern and remote, as impersonal as her father and even less interested in her feelings and thoughts. The family was Episcopalian and politically conservative. While they rarely went to church, the adults preached a strict moral code which their daughter doubted they observed.

The information noted above was elicited in our first two sessions. I had the feeling that Alice was beginning to trust me, but by our third session I was still unclear on the source of her current crisis. The family background she had described was disheartening, but it hardly seemed pathological enough to account for the girl's crying fits and general mood of despair. I was also uncomfortably aware of the fact that Alice had told me little about her relationships with her peers and particularly little about her sex life. For an attractive, twenty-year-old coed in the 1960s, that was unusual, so I decided to ask her directly. She replied, with some embarrassment, that she had plenty of acquaintances but no real friends. She was "running with a fast crowd," she said, and "would have lost my virginity, but no one asked me."

The latter remark was delivered in such a plaintive tone that I laughed out loud. Alice was laughing too, the first time, perhaps, in the three meetings we had had. She had little else to confide about sexual experiences or fantasies, but conveyed the impression that she felt less desirous than awkward. She secretly longed to experience the closeness and excitement of sexual intimacy, I imagined, but was not yet comfortable about encouraging such advances.

In our fourth meeting, Alice told me her mother and stepfather were moving to Phoenix and had insisted that she come with them. She did not want to leave Los Angeles, however, partly because she saw this as her chance to break away from her parents, but also, she implied, because she did not want to stop seeing me. Because of her refusal to accompany them, there had been a scene at home, and her mother had given her the ultimatum that they would no longer support her. As a result, she informed me, she had gone right out and applied for work at the telephone company. If it came through, she was planning to drop out of school, live on her own, and continue seeing me.

This rapid turn of events surprised me, but Alice seemed so energized, so determined and organized in her plans, that I was encouraged. I had already been impressed by her intelligence, sensitivity, and sincerity; now I saw she had spunk as well.

A few days later, I received the following letter. It was accompanied by a card that simply said, "Dear Doctor Mindess, I wrote you a story. Alice W." It seemed to me then, as it does now, expressive of the texture of her internal self at that stage of her life.

Once upon a time there was a girl. Somehow she'd managed to get herself in a terrible mess. This girl lives in her own world— she's a dreamer (of sorts). Only her own world is little. It's so little in fact she hates to be in it. Only she can't get out. She can't. And she doesn't know what to do.

Once upon a time she was born—and then she was seven. She and her mommy went on a long trip that summer because her mommy and daddy didn't love each other any more. Then she lived with her mommy for 7 more years. Her mommy found a new daddy and the little girl lived with them. Only she was afraid of her new daddy and she didn't know what her old daddy was like. Her new daddy was very good to her, and he was fair, because he didn't want to be a "stepfather" and he loved the little girl's mommy.

The mommy of this little girl tried to be a good mommy, but the little girl hated her for being so mean. The mommy used to say things that hurt the little girl and made her cry. The little girl's old daddy never said anything to her. He just sent her money because he really didn't know who she was.

THIS LITTLE GIRL TOLD LIES.

She told lies because she was afraid. The truth would have been easier to tell but she didn't know how.

One day the little girl went to college. She thought college would be lots of fun, but she was really afraid, because this little girl wasn't very smart. She didn't know how to think. She only knew how to obey, but something inside her head always made her not want to obey. So she went to college and she was very unhappy because she wasn't smart and she couldn't think and there wasn't even anyone to disobey. So she fooled around and pretended she was having a good time and acted like a big girl. She drank and laughed at jokes and went out with boys and parked and cut classes. And finally she stopped going to classes and stopped pretending and she just slept and slept and slept. She was very tired only she couldn't rest.

One day her mommy and new daddy were going to move away. The little girl was afraid she would die if she went with them, so she ran away. Now she has a new job and she lives by herself. She can see her friends all the time now—but she's started having thoughts again. And they're all unhappy thoughts.

So it's almost another 7 years and what has happened in all those years of 7? She's still a little girl, she's still dumb, she's still afraid. And it only gets worse because it's so hard to pretend.

But one thing has happened. There is one door out for her. It's a very nice man she tells all this stuff to who can figure out what it means. He figures it out and tells the little girl about it so she can change. Only she doesn't think she can change—because she has tried. Not very hard, but she has tried to force herself to change a little. And you know what? The whole mess only gets worse. And you know what else? The little girl is more afraid than ever because she doesn't know what to do and she can't do anything

and she's afraid she's going to stop talking to that man. That's
what happens when she really gets scared. She stops.

When I received this letter, I had known Alice less than a
month. I was subsequently to see her, once or twice a week, for
about 2 years. At the end of that period, a sequence of events
was to take her to live in another country. Yet she never broke
contact with me. For the next 20 years, without fail, she sent me
a letter every Christmas keeping me informed about her doings.
I am in the fortunate position, therefore, of knowing, at least in
broad outline, how the tearful, depressed young woman who consulted me when she was dropping out of college and breaking
away from her family has conducted her life into her forties. I
will report the essential facts at the end of this chapter, but first,
to set the stage for my hypothetical analyses of her case by Freud,
Jung, Skinner, Rogers, and Erickson, let me record a few dreams
she told me during our initial sessions.

The night after our first meeting, she dreamed, "I was in a
hospital because I had a cold and President Kennedy admitted
me and arranged for my accommodations. I was very weak and
kept falling down. I was put in this enormous room with a TV
and a lot of people who were sitting around talking. There was a
rug and some furniture and a lot of beds, but they weren't made.
I said something like, "I hope I won't disturb you." And there
were some parakeets in a cage, so many that they were one mass
of ruffled blue feathers." (Dream #1)

The following week, she brought in the following. "A whole
bunch of dreams. I kept waking up. One I said I must have been
bad and that's why I woke up. Later I dreamed about another
girl and a man who was The Boss. The other girl was crying. He
said something about family. I said she was old enough to account
for her own actions. My appointment with The Boss was for 9
and they kept serving meals and I had my nightgown on. He kept
whispering and I had a cold and couldn't hear him. He asked the
question like write the difference of the example that's carved on
your desk or the third line of the sideways paper." (Dream #2)

At our next appointment, she reported two dreams. "I was
talking to my father and I was sitting very far from him. I said,
'And I'm not going to your picnic either.' " (Dream #3) And,

"Three men in a car carrying books back and forth. One of them was *Franny and Zooey* and another was *Robert's Rules of Order*. A man in a wool shirt was sitting behind the steering wheel. Under the wool shirt he had on a stiff white shirt. And he said, 'I'm a very well organized person. I'm in science, you know.' I was sitting in the back handing books in and out." (Dream #4)

Finally, rounding out this series, Alice brought in the following dream when I had been seeing her for about 6 weeks. "Having dinner at your house. You were there but my conversation was with your wife. After dessert, she and your daughter were doing the dishes in a double sink with hot steamy water. I was clearing the table. I remember walking round and round. There was a child-size setting for me. Then I looked at my hand and there was a blue vein on my arm and hand. Then I was in a man's apartment and he wasn't interested in me and I wandered in and out washing my hair. The red shampoo didn't work so I tried some green shampoo. I was only wearing a robe. I thought about the man, 'He's one of those who fancies himself a great lover.' Then there was something about a razor blade at Daddy's and breaking things at 9 o'clock." (Dream #5)

## THE CASE OF ALICE W. AS TREATED BY FREUD

If Alice had consulted Sigmund Freud, he would have asked for associations to these dreams. As I did the same, let me review what she said. With regard to Dream #1, being admitted to a hospital by President Kennedy, she had a favorable view of Kennedy, admired him and thought he might bring more unity to the country. She felt attracted to the idea of being cared for in a hospital and did feel sick or she wouldn't have sought therapy in the first place. She had no associations to parakeets, but ruffled feathers suggested ruffled feelings. When I asked what the color blue brought to mind, she replied, "Well, I'm sure this doesn't mean anything, but when I was a baby my father had a blue flannel bathrobe and he used to carry me in his arms and wrap me in its folds. I can still feel the touch of the soft, warm material on my skin. I used to get up in the middle of the night when I was three or four and crawl into their bed and sleep between them. My father liked it but my mother was annoyed. I used to shave with him too. He used an old-fashioned razor and lather that he applied with a brush. He would put lather on my face too and I can still remember the feel of that brush."

Freud, I believe, would have seen in this dream and her associations to it a resounding confirmation of his oedipal theory. The very first issue her unconscious brought to light, he would have said, was her wish to be cared for by father—represented in the dream by President Kennedy—as she had been in the blissful days of her babyhood. The ruffled feathers of the parakeets he might have interpreted as mother's ruffled feelings, and the basic situation of Alice being in a hospital because she had a cold as an expression of her hope that by being unwell she would get the attention she was missing, mixed in with a dim awareness that she wasn't really all that ill. Her memories of father's blue bathrobe, the feel of it against her skin, and the feel of his shaving brush on her face would have been seen as emphasizing the sensuous nature of her lost attachment. There can be little doubt, I think, that Freud would have said that Alice at twenty was still suffering from feelings of abandonment caused by her parents' divorce and her father's subsequent emotional detachment. While I made no such interpretation, she later confirmed the Freudian view when she told me how desolate she had felt whenever her mother said (as she frequently did), "Your father doesn't love *us* anymore."

The oedipal theme, according to Freud, would have been seen as reiterated in Dream #2 in which she had an appointment with The Boss and was wearing her nightgown. The fact that he asked her a question she couldn't answer might have been related to the question of the Sphinx—the implication being that the question of our oedipal attachments is one whose answer we flinch from recognizing, as the admission of our true impulses in this area is too embarrassing for us to acknowledge.

In any case, in Dream #3, Alice's father emerges directly, but she refuses to go to his picnic. The petulant child in her, Freud would have said, was now attempting to get even with father by rejecting him as he had rejected her.

Finally, in Dream #5, having dinner at my house and talking with my wife, a Freudian view would have held that a transference of her original attachment to her father was now beginning to be projected onto me. We did not discuss this possibility at the time. Quite apart from the dream, I felt that Alice was forming a dependent attachment to me, but I wished to encourage it, or at least allow it to run its course, as our alliance seemed to give her the strength to work on her problems constructively. When I asked for her associations to this dream many years later, however, she said, "I never told you then but I had a terrible crush on you. I used to imagine how I could seduce you, cause I knew that men only wanted one thing. My mother had often warned me, 'If a man buys you dinner at 7, he'll squeeze it out of you at 11,' and had advised me, in her sardonic way, 'Keep your kisses for your husband—you'll *have* to give them to him.' I used to drive past your house to catch a glimpse of you or your family and wonder what it would be like to be your wife. The only reason we didn't have sex, I thought, was because of my integrity."

This revelation of the erotic component of the transference came as a surprise to me. Not a total surprise, I must admit, for at some level of awareness I knew there had been an attraction between us that went beyond ordinary liking and admiration. I too had felt stirrings of sexual interest in the sad, lovely girl who had come to me for help. But she was a client, barely twenty years old, and a virgin to boot. Therefore, perhaps, I did not allow myself to indulge in erotic wishes, much less to behave in a provocative manner.

In retrospect, however, it seems that a Freudian analysis of the situation would have been both accurate and enlightening. Alice could have been described as a young woman who had once been on intimate terms with her father, had lost him and been unable to replace him with a man to whom she could feel as close, and who had subsequently fallen into a state of depression from which she was trying to emerge by projecting her unresolved oedipal wishes onto the person of her therapist (i.e., me). Whether Freud would have allowed this projection to continue unchallenged is unclear, but he would have envisaged her dynamics in some such manner. Alice's estrangement from her mother would have been explained in the same formulation. Her mother may in fact have been as cold and critical as Alice portrayed her, but she was also the other member of the oedipal triangle; so the daughter's resentment must have stemmed in part from the feeling that her mother had come between her and her father—not, in this case, by monopolizing father's love, but by driving him away altogether. Add to this mother's admonitions about men as lustful beasts and we can see why the young woman was unprepared to enjoy the romantic excitement that life might have held in store.

While I did not look at Alice through Freudian eyes at the time, it seems to me now that these observations would have made a good deal of sense. So too, however, would the set of Jungian observations I am about to propose.

## —By Jung

If Alice had consulted C. G. Jung, he too would have been as interested in her dreams as in her case history and presenting problems. He too would have asked for associations to the dream material, but in addition would have amplified her personal memories with analogies drawn from mythological motifs and other forms of collective symbolism.

With respect to Dream #1, for instance, a Jungian interpretation would have held that President Kennedy's admitting Alice to the hospital represented not a disguised wish for her father to take care of her, but symbolized a unifying masculine force already at work within her unconscious. Her associations to Kennedy included the statement that he might "bring more unity to the country." Translated into her inner dynamics, Kennedy would have been seen by Jung as a positive animus figure, a powerful rational potential that could help Alice overcome her depression. The ruffled blue feathers of the parakeets in the same dream might have suggested other such lines of thought. Birds, according to mythological thinking, are messengers of the gods; they come to us from heaven, which is also most often represented by the color blue. In the Zohar and other mystical texts, blue is the color of spirit, the color of divinity. This element of Alice's dream, therefore, adds dimension to the view that spiritual forces were active within her.

In Dream #2, The Boss with whom she has an appointment at 9 asks a question "Like write the difference of the example

that's carved on your desk or the third line of the sideways paper."
A perplexing question, to say the least. While Jung might have
agreed with Freud that such questions recall the riddle of the
Sphinx, he would surely have drawn the interpretation away from
Freud's preoccupation with oedipal themes. The Sphinx's riddle,
after all, was, "What goes first on all fours, then on two, and
finally on three?"—an unfolding image of man's development and
deterioration, implying the broader existential dilemma of the
meaning of our lives. The masculine principle, in other words,
puts to the dreamer a question she cannot handle, but which she
is already feeling compelled to face. It corresponds to her initial
complaint that life seemed meaningless, that she saw herself as
a participant in "an empty, foolish charade." The number 9, on
the other hand, may refer to the beginning of the working day—
9 o'clock—or to the nine months of pregnancy. The symbolic
meaning, therefore, may have been that she was being prompted
to begin work on her unconscious material, to begin a period of
gestation that could result in her giving birth to a new attitude, a
new outlook on life.

In Dream #4, Alice is in a car carrying books back and forth.
One is *Franny and Zooey,* another *Robert's Rules of Order.* Here
the symbolism seems highly pertinent to what would have been
Jung's view of her case. Robert's rules of order refers to her need
to maintain propriety, to keep control of her emotions and impulses. As we know, however, her controls were breaking down.
She had been weeping a lot and failing her classes, felt compelled
to drop out of school, and had finally consulted me in the hope
that I could help her put herself back in order. She was, in fact,
in the same predicament that Franny went through in Salinger's
novel.

In the book, Franny suffers a nervous breakdown as a result
of becoming disillusioned with the crassness of her college environment. Her boyfriend, her teachers, the other students, and
even she herself all strike her as hopelessly entangled in their
petty egotistic strivings. "All I know is I'm losing my mind," she
cries. "I'm just sick of ego, ego, ego. My own and everybody
else's. I'm sick of everybody that wants to get somewhere, do
something distinguished and all, be somebody interesting. It's
disgusting—it is, it *is.*" She tries to help herself by reading a re-

ligious volume called *The Way of the Pilgrim* and reciting the Jesus Prayer: "Lord Jesus Christ, have mercy on me." Her efforts, however, are in vain until her brother Zooey comes to her aid. After many an inspired, ascerbic harangue, he finally tells her a story from their mutual past that breaks through her despair. It is the story of something their eldest brother, Seymour, had told him when they were all child prodigies on a radio show called, "It's a Wise Child."

Zooey had been complaining about the crassness of the radio audience, the announcer, the sponsors, and everyone connected with the show. So Seymour told him to shine his shoes. When he asked what for, Seymour told him to shine them "for the Fat Lady." At the time, Zooey tells his sister, he was thoroughly perplexed. "I didn't know what the hell he was talking about, but he had a very Seymour look on his face, and so I did it. He never did tell me who the Fat Lady was, but I shined my shoes for the Fat Lady every time I went on the air again." Then he adds— and his words become the beginning of Franny's salvation—"I'll tell you a terrible secret. Are you listening to me? *There isn't anyone out there who isn't Seymour's Fat Lady* . . . there isn't anyone anywhere that isn't Seymour's Fat Lady. Don't you know that? Don't you know that goddamned secret yet? And don't you know—*listen* to me now—*don't you know who that Fat Lady really is?* Ah buddy, ah buddy, it's Christ Himself, Christ Himself buddy."

With this theme implicit in her dream, Alice seems to have been a perfect example of Jung's contention that we fall into despair when we lose a sense of meaningfulness that goes beyond our egotistic aspirations. Her unconscious, it also seems, was prompting her to acquire a deeper, more Christlike view of the world, a view that encompasses the realization that we are all God's children, all brothers and sisters in Christ, disgusting as we may appear by more mundane standards. While I had received some training at the C. G. Jung Institute in Zurich before I became Alice's therapist, I cannot say that I made much effort to help her acquire such a view. I was no more a Jungian then than I am now—nor have I ever been deeply religious. Nevertheless, it seems convincing to me that a Jungian analysis of her predicament and a Jungian approach to treatment would have been highly appropriate—as appropriate, in its way, as a Freudian analysis would have been, too.

To compare these diverse approaches to Alice's dreams a little more fully, consider the symbolism of Dream #5. First, she is having dinner at my house, but her conversation is with my wife. Freud, as I mentioned earlier, might easily have inferred a beginning transference of the oedipal rivalry in Alice's childhood onto her relationship to me. Jung, in contrast, might have averred that the dinner was a sacramental ritual, that my wife represented my anima, and that Alice was being pulled into the magic circles of my family and my psyche. My wife and daughter doing the dishes in a double sink with hot steamy water may have represented an alchemical process of purification, while Alice's walking "round and round" the dinner table may have been interpreted as the circumambulation involved in many rituals, a preliminary form of mandala symbolism presaging the wholeness toward which she was evolving.

The blue vein Alice then saw running down her arm and hand repeats the spiritual blue of the parakeets in Dream #1, but now it is a part of her, a part of her lifeblood system. Continuing with the colors in this dream, Alice's remark about washing her hair— "The red shampoo didn't work so I tried some green shampoo"— might have been interpreted by both Freud and Jung as representing a shift from a "stop" mode to a "go" mode, or a loosening of her repressions in the context of the therapeutic relationship. The end of the dream—"I was in a man's apartment . . . I was only wearing a robe. I thought, 'He's one of those who fancies himself a great lover.' Then there was something about a razor blade at daddy's and breaking things at 9 o'clock"—seems more conducive to a Freudian than a Jungian interpretation.

The sexual implications of the shift from having dinner at my house to being in a man's apartment wearing nothing but a robe are transparent, while the sardonic thought, "He fancies himself a great lover," is reminiscent of her mother's warnings and expressive of her defensive need to scoff at the men to whom she was attracted. The razor blade may be related to her early childhood shaving ritual with daddy, while breaking things at 9 o'clock repeats the number 9 of her second dream and adds the connotations of "breaking": breaking away, breaking down, breaking free, or in other words, severing connections and controls in a maneuver Jung would have seen as a plunge into the void from which all things are born anew.

Suggestive and meaningful as these interpretations of Alice's dreams may seem to some psychologists, a therapist trained in the Skinnerian tradition would have eschewed them entirely. Not only eschewed them: the Skinnerian would have ridiculed them as highly speculative, totally unscientific, and therapeutically useless.

## —By a Behaviorist

How then would a behavior therapist have dealt with Alice as a client? In the first place, far less time would have been spent exploring the roots of her depression than Freud would have recommended, and far less time investigating the meaningfulness of her symptoms than Jung would have recommended. The symptoms themselves—crying, failing in her schoolwork, dropping out of college, withdrawal from social relations, feeling depressed, and lack of sexual activity—would have been made the focus of attention. In all probability, they would have been seen as having arisen as ways of gaining attention, and as having been reinforced by the concern, as well as the criticism, of her mother and stepfather. Her mother, furthermore, represented a negative role model, particularly with regard to sex and, more generally, in her manipulative, self-centered mode of being. Early in the therapy, however—from the very first session, in fact—a behavior therapist would have had Alice concentrate not on what had made her unhappy but on what might begin to make her happy.

Such a therapist might have had her start by listing her problems in order of severity. Which of your symptoms, the behaviorist might have asked, seems to you most amenable to change? Which seems the hardest for you to do anything about? Having secured such a list, this therapist would have helped her work on her problems, one by one, in a systematic fashion. Let us suppose that the problem Alice would have thought she could most readily attack was her crying. Up to now she had been conceiving of it as uncontrollable, crying spells that came upon her "out of the blue," so to speak. The therapist might have suggested two interlocking ways of dispelling this notion. First, he might have taught Alice certain techniques of relaxation—breathing exercises, methods of muscular relaxation, autosuggestions like "I'm feeling calm, there's nothing to be afraid of, nothing hurts me, I don't have to cry"—and perhaps recommended baths or showers, taking walks, or soothing herself in other ways when she felt a crying spell coming on.

Second, the therapist might have taught her to observe the conditions under which she felt like crying. Far from occurring as spontaneously as she imagined, her crying, she would have discovered, was governed by external and internal stimuli. In the presence of certain people, perhaps, from whom she could expect sympathy, or when she engaged in a line of thought—say, about her father's detachment or her mother's coldness—the tears would well up. Refraining from those thoughts, therefore, or avoiding contact with those people could reduce the incidence of her crying spells. More important, in carrying out such observations she would have learned that she could indeed exert control over her tears, if not directly, then by controlling the conditions that caused them. Implicit in this learning would have been the dawning awareness that she could exert control over her other problems as well, that she was not so much a victim of circumstance or the plaything of mysterious forces as a rational being who could make her experiences more conducive to her welfare.

One of Skinner's most central concepts is contained in the term, "contingencies of reinforcement." "Behavior," he has said, "is maintained by its consequences." Applied to Alice's case, these phrases propose that the consequences of her crying, failing, withdrawing, feeling depressed, and refraining from sex kept her doing these things, and that the reinforcements she was receiving were effective in very specific ways—probably by occurring immediately after each display of her problem behavior. To cure her, therefore, would require careful scrutiny of the ways in which her problem behavior was being reinforced, followed by interventions designed to break up these negative patterns.

Let us imagine, for instance, that she had come to the place in her list where she wished to overcome her sexual problem. Recall that she had said to me, "I would have lost my virginity, but no one asked me"—a wistful statement indicating that she was, in this area, as in so many others, a pawn in the hands of other people's desires. But what really went on between her and eligible young men? Did they make passes that she rejected, seductive remarks that she failed to respond to? It was hard for me to believe that no one had ever been interested in her sexually, for she was a very attractive young woman, exuding, in my presence at least, an air of repressed but discernible passion. Perhaps, then, her modus vivendi was to derive satisfaction by frustrating men's sexual desires, seeing that hopeful look in their eyes subdued by her unresponsiveness.

If that were the case, the problem would be difficult to dissolve, as it would have been promoted more by what she wasn't doing than by what she was doing. Nevertheless, it would not be impossible. Alice would have had to learn, through her own candid observations, precisely what she was getting in the form of immediate rewards from the men she was ignoring, and this need have been nothing more than the satisfaction of seeing their disappointment. She then would have had to face the question whether it was worthwhile to deprive herself of sexual gratification in order to enjoy the discomfiture of her rejected suitors. It would be hoped that she would have decided to give up the old self-defeating pattern in favor of a newer, more normal one.

Would these techniques have been helpful in Alice's case? If she had been willing to cooperate with such an approach, they probably would have yielded results—not in alleviating her alienated outlook as much as in eliminating her specific symptoms, but that in turn might have led to greater optimism. I cannot, however, claim that I employed them to any great extent. No more a behaviorist than a Freudian or Jungian, I treated Alice with a mishmash of empathy, suggestions, reflections, interpretations, and wordless receptivity that in my more high-falutin' moments I call "eclectic therapy."

## —By Rogers

In any case, what would Carl Rogers have done if Alice had consulted him? Based on the published transcripts of his work with other clients, we might have anticipated something resembling the following:

*Session 1*

A: I have come to see you because I've been very depressed. I cry a lot for no reason at all, and I just don't care about anything anymore.

R: You've really been feeling down. You shed many tears, though you don't even know what you're crying about, and you've lost all your interests, too.

A: That's right. I haven't been doing my schoolwork, my grades are terrible, and the people I've been hanging out with all seem like jerks. They're so rah-rah, you know, and maybe I should be too, but I don't care. I don't care about anything.

R: You've said that several times now. You're really emphasizing that feeling that nothing matters, that nothing holds your interest. You can't get involved in your schoolwork or the college-type things your friends get excited about. Some part of you thinks that you should be like them, though.

A: Well, it does seem strange, doesn't it? After all, shouldn't a normal person like to go to parties and football games and make out with boys? I know my parents think there's something wrong with me.

R: You don't feel normal because you don't like to do what the other students seem to enjoy so much. And apparently your parents share that opinion.

A: It's more complicated than that. My mother wouldn't approve of what the other kids do, if she knew what they really do. And what I've done too. I mean drinking and smoking dope. As far as sex goes, though, I'm doing just like she taught me. I mean nothing. But I don't think that's normal. Do you?

R: Now you wonder if I think you're normal since you're not having sexual relations. And your mother might approve of that, but she surely wouldn't condone your drinking and smoking marijuana.

A: I'm all mixed up. I don't know what's right or wrong, I think I hate her for being so mean, and my father doesn't even care. Ever since he left us, he just sent money, but otherwise he doesn't know I exist.

R: It is confusing, isn't it. Your mother strikes you as mean, your father sends money for your support but he doesn't take an interest in how you're feeling or what you're doing, and you yourself can't think things through clearly right now.

A: To tell you the truth, I've given up. I feel so miserable that I just want to curl up and die.

R: So under your confusion there's a lot of despair. You feel defeated, and rather than try to fight it anymore, sometimes you'd just like to give up entirely.

A: Yes. (She cries.) Damn them! Damn them both. My mom always tells me what to do—what not to do, rather—only her advice is so stupid, she doesn't know who I am, she doesn't have the slightest idea, and if she did, she'd be shocked. And my dad doesn't care, he doesn't care at all, and yet he's a nice man, he really is, and I used to love him so much. (Cries again.)

R: Now you're really getting in touch with your deeper feelings, and there's so much there you can barely contain it all. You're angry at them both, sometimes you hate them, and yet you love them too. Or at least you love your dad. But your mother doesn't understand you at all. And if she did, she'd never approve.

A: Well, would you? Would you approve of a daughter who resents you and lies to you and doesn't do her work and stays in bed all day and cries?

R: Again you're concerned about what I might think of you. Other people's opinions mean a lot to you—what your mother thinks or might think, your father, your friends, and now me.

A: I guess I should start thinking more for myself. Not caring so much (she laughs)—huh, that's funny, I came in here telling you I don't care about anything, and now it seems I care too much. About them, I mean. About everyone else and what they think of me. That's dumb! I should try figuring out where *I* stand, what *I* approve of in myself, what *I* want to do with my life. It's so hard though, I don't know where to begin.

R: It *is* hard to think for yourself, especially when you haven't been in the habit of doing it. You have so many different feelings and so many different thoughts, and some of them seem contradictory and some of them seem not too nice. And yet they're all you, they're all parts of you, and how do you put them all together and decide what you want to do . . .

   If I have represented Rogers accurately, we may see in this

vignette the rudiments of the processes his approach to therapy usually engenders. If you stay with the feelings a person brings in, he has said, receive them empathically and reflect them accurately, the person will move to an expression of deeper feelings, when ready. If you stay with those feelings in the same way, getting every nuance and accepting the complexity of the person's being, he or she will move toward insight into the patterns of his or her experience. If you stay with this emerging insight and respect its validity, the person will begin to engage in constructive action. Rogers also has made the point that his clients move away from judging themselves through others' eyes toward accepting themselves for who they are.

Both these processes, I imagine, would have taken place in Alice if she had consulted him. Beyond that, as the therapy proceeded, she probably would have become more congruent with her organismic self, which would have included a greater acceptance of her sexuality as well as her social needs, without denying her awareness of the superficiality that is often a part of social relations. In time, her depression probably would have lifted, her withdrawal and alienation would have diminished, and she would have assumed a more authentic, and therefore more satisfying way of conducting her life.

## —BY ERICKSON

How interesting, then, that this young woman probably would have been helped by Milton Erickson, too. If she had consulted him, the treatment she would have received would have been notably different than that provided by Rogers (not to speak of Freud, Jung, or a Skinnerian). If Alice had begun by telling him that she was crying a lot and thinking of dropping out of college, that she was taking incompletes or failing every course, and that the social life she had been pursuing seemed meaningless and foolish, he would have listened closely. As she spoke about her parents—how cold and critical her mother was, how her father had left and seemed not to care about her anymore—he would have observed her body language, the droop of her shoulders, the way she twisted her hands. As she developed her portrait of the emptiness of her life, the lack of love and understanding in her childhood, and confided, in her wistful way, that she was still a virgin, he would have become as attuned to what she was *not* saying as to what she was.

Finally, perhaps, he might have said, "Young lady, I think you're right. Life has been so unfair to you, with those uncaring parents, those superficial friends, that your dropping out is probably the smartest thing you can do. I mean, what's the point of trying when nobody understands and nobody gives a damn. Of course you're crying a lot. You're grieving over all those wasted years, and whenever we review our unhappiness, tears come to our eyes. But I think you should do it more. Do it fully. Not just a couple of times a day, but all day long. All night too, if you can stay awake. Cry it out. Cry it out completely, and then take off. Make a total break with your parents, drop out of school, and leave. Leave this town and don't look back."

Had Erickson taken this tack, Alice might well have become confused. Not at all what she would have expected a psychotherapist to suggest, she might have knitted her brows and wondered if Dr. Erickson was putting her on. But why would he do such a thing? What could he be getting at? In any case, his recommendations would have been far more radical than the way she was actually feeling. Besides, she might have resented his authoritarian tone. Telling her what to do, just like that—why, he barely knew her, and it was *her* life, not his, so who was he to tell her how to live it?

With some of the spunk she was later to display in response to her mother's ultimatum, Alice might have told Erickson that his advice was off target. She didn't want to cry all day; she didn't want to cry at all. And as for leaving town, where would she go? What would she do without her friends and her classes and even her stupid parents?

At this point, Erickson might have made a sudden switch. "Let me tell you a story," he might have said. "A true story. About myself. I understand you because, as you see (pointing to his wheelchair and his paralyzed legs), life has also been unfair to me. I had polio twice, you know. First when I was a teenager, just a little younger than you, and then again in my early fifties. It left me paralyzed, the first time, from the neck down. And I gave up too. I thought, goddamn it—yes, I swore to myself about my affliction—goddamn it, this is not right! I didn't do anything to deserve this. And I won't accept it. I won't put up with it. I'm just going to close my eyes and say to hell with everything and everybody, and refuse to eat, and just lie here until I die. That's what I'm going to do." Then, looking at Alice with a total poker face, he might have added, "And that's exactly what I did."

"No, you didn't," Alice would have replied. "You became a doctor. Somehow you got well enough to go to medical school, and you learned to take care of yourself, and got married, and had all those kids, and, and . . . gosh, how did you stand it when the polio hit you again?"

"The same way you stood it, I suppose, when your daddy left, and your mom was mean, and you found yourself taking a bunch of useless courses and hanging out with a bunch of jerky friends."

I know, of course, that the way I have imagined Erickson, Rogers, and the rest dealing with Alice are only rough approximations of what they would have done. Each of them, were he to have read my depiction of himself, would have corrected if not chastised me, and been fully justified in doing so. The point I am trying to make, however, does not depend on total verisimilitude in these sketches. All I want to demonstrate is that there would have been major differences in the ways the psychologists I have discussed in this book would have viewed and treated the same case.

And what of it? What would their different views of Alice have implied? And what would have been the results of their distinctive approaches?

To take these questions in order, the great psychologists' explanations of any individual's problems may be likened to the fabled blind men's descriptions of the elephant. (The first, you will recall, said the creature resembled a pillar; the second said it was more like a rope with a tassel on the end; the third described it as a thick, writhing snake, while the fourth said it was a massive slab.) In other words, each psychologist may accurately describe what he encounters, but each encounters a different aspect of the individual in front of him.

As far as the effectiveness of their treatments is concerned, consulting any one of them, I believe, would have been beneficial to Alice. As I tried to indicate in my sketches, each one would have helped her in his own way, but each one probably would have helped her. That is, if she had been ready to be helped. As it happens, she was—for she even made progress in treatment with me.

## —BY THE AUTHOR

I continued seeing Alice for about 2 years. As I have already indicated, my approach was eclectic. In those days, I often thought along Freudian and Jungian lines, but my therapeutic style was most like Rogers', in the sense of being primarily supportive, non-directive, and non-judgmental. (At least, that's how I remember it. Alice, on the other hand, recently told me that she recalls my being more directive and interpretive than I think I was. Her remark gave me food for thought. Not only does our memory play tricks on us, but our definition of what we are doing now, as well as what we did in the past, is colored by concepts we maintain of the kinds of therapists we are. Were we to ask our clients how they perceive us, we might be surprised to find that their assessment of our supportiveness, empathy, confrontiveness, and insightfulness is often different than our own.) In any case, the rapport established between Alice and me was very strong (we both agree to that), and Alice's crying diminished considerably after the first few months. To my surprise, she severed relations with her mother and stepfather, then began to make tentative overtures to her natural father. He responded in time, and there were some touching moments when they recalled their early closeness and professed their love for each other despite their years of estrangement. Alice dropped out of college, but continued to work for the phone company. She made some new friends and eventually met a man to whom she was attracted. Her alienated outlook gave way to a more hopeful attitude. I would not say she became a joyous person, but she did emerge from depression to a sense of increasing satisfaction with herself and her life.

Around the time she decided to terminate her therapy, Alice married and moved to Canada. In the 20-odd years since then, she has raised a son, divorced, and remarried. Ten years ago, she returned to college to complete her undergraduate work. That accomplished, she decided to study psychology. She recently received her Ph.D. and specializes in treating people suffering from depression.

Her unbroken correspondence with me over all these years may be seen as evidence of an unresolved transference, as our initial rapport may be seen as deriving from her need for an attentive male figure and my predilection, perhaps, for helping damsels in distress. I would not contest the validity of such explanations, but the matter also comes down to the fact that Alice and I liked each other from the start. There was a meeting of minds—I hesitate to say of souls—that went beyond the words we exchanged, beyond the formal roles we played in each other's lives. It was natural, therefore, for her to want to keep in contact, and one of the many things I admire in her to this day is her penchant for acting as her heart dictates. She is not an impulsive person—far from it—but she has a way of deciding that she really wants to do something *and doing it* that is quite remarkable. To use some crude expressions, she puts her money where her mouth is, her cards on the table, her ass on the line. She is an unusually sincere and genuine human being, and the fact that she trusted me to treat her 20 years ago and has enough faith in me now to allow me to use her case to illustrate my thesis evokes my gratitude. Thank you, dear. If you are reading these words, I hope my speculations and observations have proved worthy of your trust.

1.  This study is based on the case of a former client of mine, a woman who was kind enough to allow me to use the data of her life to illustrate the application of the theories and techniques discussed in this book. It is, however, a somewhat fictionalized account, with enough identifying information changed to protect the anonymity of the subject.

# 8

# Conclusion

## Psychology as a Human Undertaking

### A RESTATEMENT OF MY THESIS: ITS IMPLICATIONS

If the making of psychology is highly influenced by the personal characteristics of its makers, what can we conclude about the field as a whole? If theories of personality are based on the personalities of the theorists who created them, methods of psychotherapy based on the problems and resolutions of the therapists who devised them, what can we believe, whom can we trust?

Believe all intelligent theorists and trust all sincere therapists, I would say—*up to a point*. The fact that a theorist's insights derive in part from his own peculiarities, that a therapist's techniques may have been used on himself, does not invalidate them. Whether they will prove enlightening and beneficial to you is another question, but one way to find out is to try them out.

The conclusions we should reach about the field as a whole, however, must begin with a recognition of the subjective element in all personality theories, the limited applicability of all therapeutic techniques, and proceed to the relativity of psychological truth. They should apply, moreover, not just to the leaders of the field, but to all psychologists, famous or unknown, and to each and every one of us as we try to understand ourselves and each other, try to help ourselves and each other.

To say that psychological truth and psychotherapeutic effectiveness are relative may seem banal, for who would deny that every theory applies more to some people than to others, that every system of psychotherapy helps some people more than others? Only the most fervent proponents of an approach claim universal validity for it in an overt way. Covertly, however, we all cleave to favorite belief systems, employ typical ways of trying to help, and cannot rid ourselves of the notion that what seems right to us should apply to others too.

I say "cannot," but perhaps we can. With a little effort, perhaps we can see that, just as certain foods agree with me but not with you, that a particular diet will put weight on one person but not on another, therapeutic techniques must vary in the benefits they can deliver to different individuals, and that that variance must include the possibility that they may not benefit certain individuals at all.

As I tried to indicate in my fanciful treatment of Alice W. by Freud, Jung, Rogers, Erickson, and a behavior therapist, many kinds of treatment can be beneficial if the sufferer cooperates and has a strong enough desire to get well. But what does that suggest regarding the validity of each therapeutic system's assumptions? Is each one partially correct, correct at a different level, or is there an element common to all that has little to do with the assumptions of the practitioners?

Perhaps the mere fact that a person designated as a professional psychotherapist pays attention to the sufferer, takes time to listen to him and puts forth energy in an effort to help is all it takes. Perhaps the crucial element in psychotherapy is the reformulation of the client's suffering and confusion into some sort of meaningful pattern that lends significance to his distress and points to a way beyond it, regardless of the form that significance and way may take. On the other hand, perhaps there *is* a cluster of unconscious dynamics to unearth, a spiritual dimension to accept, a set of reinforcements to modify, a need to get in touch with one's organismic self, a reservoir of unrecognized strength to tap. Perhaps, too, there is an area of pain only time can heal in everyone's personal misery. In the aggregate, they all seem possible although, in individual cases, one approach may be more accurate than another.

It remains to be seen, however, if the formulations that apply most accurately to a given individual are a function of preexisting fact or explanatory choice. The sufferer, I would suggest, feels a need to find *some* way out of his suffering. If he comes to believe it is due to unconscious factors that have to be exposed, then that may become that person's pathway to health. If he chooses to believe it is due to a need for spiritual growth or lack of congruence with his true self, then either of those may become that person's road to salvation. What I am proposing is that we each play a crucial part in creating our own deliverance by subscribing to a particular belief system, much as religious adherents choose to have faith in certain sets of teachings, political activists to support particular social doctrines.

I do not point out the pattern to attack it, however. The only thing wrong with subscribing to specific explanatory formulas and therapeutic systems is denying that we have done so, for such denial can lead to the righteousness of the "true believer," the self-congratulatory delusion that one has found The Way instead of *a* way.

There are approximately 100,000 psychotherapists plying their trade in this country at present. If we could envision them all at once, in their offices and clinics, interviewing people young and old, some searching and eager, some desperate and confused, some resistant and blasé, the panorama would be touching, impressive, discouraging, and ironic: touching, because of the intimate, tender feelings that are regularly exposed; impressive, because through talk alone lives and sanity are being saved; discouraging, because so many who come for help do not improve very much; and ironic, because the practitioners, for all their experience and training, are sometimes as troubled as their clients.

These observations on the workings of psychotherapy lead to the broader question of the validity of personality theory. Since many such theories coexist, each claiming to explain what makes us think, feel, and act as we do, can they all be equally true? Are they all, perhaps, equally false? Or is there some way in which one may be truer of you, another truer of me, another truer overall, and yet another more erroneous than the rest?

To put it more fundamentally, what does make us think, feel, and act as we do? What causes each of us to seek certain goals, find happiness in certain ways, or fail to find happiness and become entrapped in frustrating patterns of living? What makes us tick and what makes us sick? That dual question is what the psychology of personality is all about; that, and the related issue of individual differences. Why are your goals and preferences not the same as mine? What determines each person's unique set of values, attitudes, and problems?

It was when I was a young man, newly Ph.D.'d, that I came across Kluckhohn and Murray's observation, earlier quoted, that in some respects every person is like all other persons, in some respects like some other persons, and in some respects like no other person. Impressed by the neatness of the formula, I tried to flesh it out. The ways in which we are all alike, I surmised, include the fact that we all have security needs, sex drives, power motives, cravings for attention and recognition, for self-expression and self-actualization. If those needs and drives are unsatisfied, we feel frustrated and unfulfilled. The ways in which we are each like some other persons, I thought, come down to the fact that women share certain experiences and resultant outlooks with other women, men with other men, that those of one generation experience the world somewhat differently than those of another generation, that members of a particular family, a particular ethnic group, a particular socioeconomic stratum share characteristics with their confrères, that introverts are more like other introverts than they are like extroverts, and so on. The ways in which we are each unique, however, intrigued me most of all, but it was that category that seemed most refractory to explication.

It still does. Over all the years I have been in the field, I have neither come across nor come up with a cogent explanation of the incontestable uniqueness of each and every individual on the face of the globe. On that account, perhaps, I began to develop the skeptical viewpoint that has informed this book, the view that psychology is an all-too-human undertaking, limited in general by the limitations we share in common and limited in its parts by the limitations of the creators of those parts. To portray psychology as a human undertaking is not to deride it, however. I personally find it heartening that bumbling efforts can produce results, that despite their limitations, psychologists can understand us to some extent and help us much of the time.

What is true of psychology and psychologists, moreover, is true of humanity as a whole. We are all locked into our own heads and hearts. We all see the world through the windows of our own eyes and interpret our perceptions in the light and darkness of our own experience. That we can understand and help each other to whatever extent we do is remarkable and inspiring. To imagine that we are capable of complete or nearly complete help and understanding, however, is nothing less than hubris—and ironically, some of our greatest geniuses have been most guilty of this sin.

Well, you know the rest. I went from bad to worse. Having adopted the relativistic stance I have been belaboring in these pages, I began to succumb to the temptation to preach it to students and colleagues. I have done that shamelessly for years, but fully admit that my standpoint is as limited as any other. This realization has led me to conclude that I must end this work on an anticlimactic note, or to put it more generously, in a minor key. Let me, therefore, repeat the bad taste I exhibited in the beginning, by quoting myself in the form of another poem I wrote a few years ago. It is entitled, "Perhaps," and sums up my stance as well as anything I could say in prose.

When I was young and full of piss,
When I was sharp and sure,
When I knew That as well as This
And all my thoughts ran pure—

Then I said, "Right!" and I said, "Wrong!"
And I extolled The Way.
My arguments were like a song
That I could sing all day.

But now I'm old and full of doubt.
My thoughts are rent with gaps.
Uncertain how things come about,
I sadly say, "Perhaps."

And saying that, am I now wise?
Have I now seen the truth?

Can I now rest my weary eyes
And wait for eager youth

To come and beg me answer this:
"Does Wisdom say Perhaps?"
So I, though old, still full of piss,
Can smile and say, "Perhaps."

# References

Brome, V. *Jung: Man and myth*. New York: Atheneum, 1981.

Clark, R. W. *Freud: The man and the cause*. New York: Random House, 1980.

Diamond, S., in Rieber, R. W., Wilhelm Wundt and the Making of a Scientific Psychology, New York, Plenum Press, 1980.

Elms, A. C. Skinner's dark year and *Waldon Two*. *American Psychologist*, May 1981, pp. 470–479.

Evans, R. *Carl Rogers: The man and his ideas*. New York: Dutton, 1975.

Haley, J. *Conversations with Milton H. Erickson*. New York: Triangle, 1985.

Havens, R. A. *The wisdom of Milton H. Erickson*. New York: Irvington, 1985.

James, W. *Psychology: The briefer course*. New York: Harper, 1961.

James, W. *The varieties of religious experience*. New York: Macmillan, 1961.

Jones, E. *The life and work of Sigmund Freud*. New York: Basic Books, 1961.

Jung, C. G. *Memories, dreams, reflections*. New York: Random House, 1961.

Kirschenbaum, H. *On becoming Carl Rogers*. New York: Dell, 1979.

Kubly, H. *Native's return*. Stein & Day, Scarborough, NY: 1981.

Matthiessen, F. O. *The James family*. New York: Knopf, 1947.

Miller, G. & Buckhout, R. *Psychology: The science of mental life*. Harper, 1973.

Monte, C. *Beneath the mask*. New York: Holt, Rinehart, & Winston, 1980.

Perry, R. B. *The thought and character of William James*. Boston: Little Brown, 1935.

Roazen, P. *Freud and his followers*. New York: Knopf, 1975.

Rogers, C. R. *On becoming a person*. Boston: Houghton Mifflin, 1961.

Rogers, C. R. *A way of being*. Boston: Houghton Mifflin 1980.

Rosen, S. *My voice will go with you: The teaching tales of Milton H. Erickson*. New York: Norton, 1982.

Rossi, E. (Ed.). *Collected papers of Milton H. Erickson*. Irvington, 1980.

Rossi, E., et al. *Healing in hypnosis*. New York: Irvington, 1983.

Salinger, J. D. *Frannie and Zooey*. Boston: Little Brown, 1961.

Schur, M. *Freud: Living and dying*. NY: Int. U. Press, 1972.

Skinner, B. F. *Walden two*. New York: Macmillan, 1948.

Skinner, B. F. *Science and human behavior*. New York: Macmillan, 1953.

Skinner, B. F. *Particulars of my life*. New York: Knopf, 1976.

Skinner, B. F. *The shaping of a behaviorist*. New York: Knopf, 1979.

Skinner, B. F. *A matter of consequences*. New York: Knopf, 1983.

Sorell, W. *The Swiss*. New York: Bobbs-Merrill, 1972.

Stolorow, R. D., & Atwood, G. E. *Faces in a cloud*. New York: Jason Aronson, 1979.

Strouse, J. *Alice James: A biography*. Boston: Houghton Mifflin, 1980.

# Index

*About Behaviorism* (Skinner), 102
Adler, Alfred, 82
  and Freud, 56
  and inferiority-superiority dy-
    namics, 45
  and the unconscious, 56
Aldridge, John W., 23
Allen, Frederick, 119
Allport, Gordon, 43
*Answer to Job* (Jung), 83n
Archetypes, Jungian, 77–78, 122
Arnold, Walter, 104
Atwood, G. E., 51, 63
Autohypnosis, 134, 135–137

Baby tender, 97, 102
*Becoming Partners* (Rogers), 125
Behaviorism, 13, 14, 86, 92–104,
  105–106, 107

in case study, 159–161
contributions of, 107
critics of, 85, 98, 102,
  103–104
*Behaviorism* (Watson), 92
Berman, Louis, 92, 94
Bettelheim, Bruno, 48
*Beyond Freedom and Dignity*
  (Skinner), 94, 98, 102
Bismark, Otto von, 30, 31
Brice, Norman, 128
Brücke, Ernst, 56

C. G. Jung Institute (Zurich), 18–
  19, 25, 68, 71, 80–81, 157
Carotenuto, Aldo, 83n
*Carl Rogers* (Rogers), 125
*Carl Rogers on Encounter Groups*
  (Rogers), 125

*Carl Rogers on Personal Power* (Rogers), 125
Cartwright, Rosalind Dymond, 128
Center for Studies of the Person, 126
Charcot, Jean-Martin, 56–57
Chomsky, Noam, 85, 98, 103–104
Clark, R. W., 48, 54, 58
*Clinical Treatment of the Problem Child, The* (Rogers), 119
Clinicians, vs. researchers, 12
Compulsiveness, 34
Conditioned reflex, 92
Conditioning, operant, 94–96
   vs. Pavlovian, 95
Consciousness
   Jamesian, 40
      vs. Wundt, 44
   Jungian, 78
*Contingencies of Reinforcement* (Skinner), 102
*Counseling and Psychotherapy* (Rogers), 120, 121
*Cumulative Record* (Skinner), 102

Dreams, 53, 69–70, 79, 80–81
   in case study, 151–154, 155–159

Elms, Alan C., 104–105
Emerson, Ralph Waldo, 36, 41, 78
*Enantiodromia*, 76
Erickson, Milton, 17, 25, 132–144
   and autohypnosis, 134, 135–137, 142
   biography of, 134–138
   and case study, 164–166
   and directiveness, 132–133, 134
   and hypnotherapy, 133
   and mastery of pain, 142
   personality of, 138, 139, 143

and religion, 143
and Rogers, 112, 132, 143–144, 145
therapeutic techniques of, 141–142, 143, 144
Existentialism, 12, 13

Farson, Richard, 128
Fliess, Wilhelm, 53, 55, 62–63
Flüss, Gisela, 54
Francis Joseph, Emperor of Austria-Hungary, 48
*Freedom to Learn* (Rogers), 125, 127
Freud, Amalie, 49, 50–51
Freud, John, 49–50
Freud, Martha Bernays, 55, 63
Freud, Sigmund, 14, 15, 16, 19, 25, 47–65
   biography of, 48–58
   and case study, 152–155
   defense mechanisms in, 60
   and the ego, 59
   humor in, 51, 59
   influences on, 56–57
   and Jung, 47, 56, 66, 68, 76, 77, 80, 81–82, 83$n$
   and Oedipus complex, 45, 51–53, 61
   development of, 63
   and psychoanalysis, 60, 61–62, 64, 65
   and religion, 50, 59
   and self-analysis, 53–54
   and sexuality, 13, 23, 43, 46, 55, 57, 60–61, 63–64, 68
   and sublimation, 55, 61, 63
   temperament of, 57–59, 64, 65
   and the unconscious, 56–57, 60
   writings of, 50–51, 54, 55, 62
   and Wundt, 11

Fromm, Erich, 82, 98, 108
Frost, Robert, 91, 104, 105
*Future of an Illusion, The* (Freud),
    50

Gendlin, Eugene, 124
Germany, in the 19th century, 30
Guilt
    and religion, 50
    and sibling rivalry, 52, 53

Haley, Jay, 134
Havens, Ronald A., 134
Horney, Karen, 82
Humor, study of, 19, 81
Huxley, Julian, 85, 98
Hypnosis, 56; *see also* Autohyp-
    nosis
Hysteria, 55, 56, 57

Individuation, 76, 77
Industrial revolution, 30
*Interpretation of Dreams, The*
    (Freud), 51, 54, 55, 63
Introspection, as mental exercise,
    32–33

Jacobi, Jolande, 67–68, 74
James, Alice Gibbons, 40, 43
James, Henry (father of William
    and Henry), 35, 37, 39,
    41–43
James, Henry, 37, 39, 41–42
James, William, 25–26, 33–44
    biography of, 36–43
    depression in, 37–38, 44
    and free will, 38–39, 44
    personality of, 29

religious feeling in, 41–42, 43
    and sex, 43–44
    teaching style of, 28
    writings of, 37–38, 39
Jones, Ernest, 48, 50, 55, 58
Jung, Carl Gustav, 14, 15, 25, 65–
    82
    and archetypes, 77–78, 122
    biography of, 67, 68–76
    and case study, 155–159
    and collective unconscious, 77–
        78
    and concept of Self, 78–79, 83n
    dreams of, 69–70, 78, 79
    and Freud, 76, 81–82
    and introversion–extroversion,
        45, 76, 77
    and paradox, 66, 74
    personality of, 67, 74, 78
        dual, 74, 77
    and religion, 72–73
    writings of, 65–66, 72
Jung, Emma Rauschenbach,
    75–76
*Jung and the Story of Our Time*
    (Van der Post), 83n

Kiesler, Donald, 124–125
Kirschenbaum, Howard, 113,
    115, 120, 126, 128
Klopfer, Bruno, 18
Kluckhohn, Clyde, 46, 172
Krafft-Ebing, Richard von, 75
Kubly, Herbert, 67

*Lehrbuch der Psychiatrie* (Krafft-
    Ebing), 75
Leipzig, University of, 11, 30–31
*Lie Down in Darkness* (Styron),
    24

Maslow, Abraham, 45
Masson, Jeffrey, 48
*Matter of Consequences, A*
    (Skinner), 85, 108
Mead, Margaret, 85, 98
Meador, Bruce, 128
*Memories, Dreams, Reflections*
    (Jung), 71
*Modern Man in Search of a Soul*
    (Jung), 66
Monte, Christopher, 52
*Moses and Monotheism* (Freud),
    50, 55
Murray, Henry, 46, 172
Murry, John Middleton, 15, 145
*My Voice Will Go with You* (Ro-
    sen), 138, 141

New York City, in 19th century,
    35–36
New York State, in 19th century,
    36
Nietzsche, Friedrich, 15

Oedipus complex, 45, 51–53, 61,
    63, 122, 153, 154
*On Becoming a Person* (Rogers),
    125
*On the Psychology and Patholo-
    gy of So-Called Occult Phe-
    nomena* (Jung), 74
*On the Psychology of the Uncon-
    scious* (Jung), 83n

Particulars of My Life (Skinner),
    85
Pavlov, Ivan, 92, 93, 95
Perls, Frederick, 21

Personality theory, 171–172
    of Freud, 60–61, 62, 64
    of Jung, 66, 76
    schools of, 12, 81–82
    sources of, 45–47
    subjective elements in, 169
*Philosophy* (Russell), 92
Piaget, Jean, 47
*Place of the Sciences of Man in
    the System of Sciences, The*
    (Piaget), 47
Popper, Karl, 85, 98
*Principles of Psychology, The*
    (James), 40–41, 43
Project Pigeon, 96–97
Projection, 91
Psychoanalysis, 60, 61–62, 64, 65,
    82n
Psychobiography, 23–24, 25
*Psychological Types* (Jung), 76
*Psychology of Dementia Praecox*
    (Jung), 76
*Psychopathology of Everyday
    Life, The* (Freud), 55

Rank, Otto, 82, 119
    and Freud, 56
Reich, Wilhelm, 82
*Religion Called Behaviorism, The*
    (Berman), 94
Researchers, vs. clinicians, 12
Roazen, P., 48, 53, 58–59
Rogers, Carl, 17, 20, 25, 111–132
    biography of, 112–127, 130–131
    and case study, 161–164
    and client-centered counseling,
        111, 120, 132
    contrasted with other psycholo-
        gists, 131–132
    and Erickson, 143–144, 145

and human potential move-
    ment, 124, 126
humor in, 129–130
personality of, 117, 128–130,
    131
and psychoanalysis, 118
and religion, 114–118
and schizophrenia project, 125
and scientific objectivity, 111,
    122
and Skinner, 85, 98
writings of, 119, 123, 125, 127
Rogers, Helen Elliott, 117, 118,
    119–120, 125, 126
Rogers, Julia, 113–114
Rogers, Walter, 113, 114–115
Rorschach technique, 18
Rosen, Sidney, 139, 141
Rossi, Ernest, 134, 135, 138, 144
Russell, Bertrand, 92


Schopenhauer, Arthur, 57
*Science and Human Behavior*
    (Skinner), 95, 102
Scranton, Pennsylvania, 90, 104,
    105, 108
*Secret Symmetry, A* (Carotenu-
    to), 83
Seduction theory, Freud's, 63
Self, Jungian concept of, 78–79,
    83*n*
Self-actualization, 45
Sennett, Richard, 104
Sexuality
    in case study, 154, 160–161
    and Freud, 13, 23, 43, 46, 55
    infantile, 55, 61, 62
    and James, 43–44
    and Reich, 82*n*
    and the Swiss, 67–68

*Shaping of a Behaviorist, The*
    (Skinner), 85
Skinner, B. F., 14, 16, 21, 25,
    84–109
    and baby tender, 97
    and behaviorism, 13, 86, 92–
    104, 105–106, 107
    biography of, 84–98
    critics of, 85, 98, 102, 103–104
    defense mechanisms in, 91, 105
    and free will, 94, 103
    personality of, 106–107
    and religion, 88
    and sexuality, 89–90
    and teaching machines, 97–98
    writings of, 85, 89–91, 93–95,
    99–104
Skinner, Yvonne Blue, 89, 90
"Skinner box," 96
Spielrein, Sabina, 83*n*
Stolorow, R. D., 51, 63
Strouse, Jean, 43
*Studies in Hysteria* (Freud &
    Breuer), 62
*Studies in Word Association*
    (Jung), 76
Styron, William, 24
Sublimation, 55, 61, 63
Swedenborg, Emanuel, 37
Swiss, national traits of, 67–68
Symbolism, 155–156, 158
*Symbols of Transformation*
    (Jung), 83*n*
Synchronicity, 75


Taft, Jessie, 119
*Technology of Teaching, The*
    (Skinner), 102
*Therapeutic Relationship and Its
    Input, The*, 125

Tomlinson, T. M., 128
*Totem and Taboo* (Freud), 50
Transpersonalists, 12
Truax, Charles, 124, 125

Unconscious
  and Adler, 56
  and Freud, 56–57
  and Jung, 56, 66, 68, 71, 77–78
    collective, 77–78
    healing power of, 71, 83n

Van der Post, Laurens, 83n
*Varieties of Religious Experience,
  The* (James), 41, 42, 43
Vienna, in the 19th century, 48–
  49

*Walden Two* (Skinner), 94, 98,
  99–102, 108–109
Watson, John, 92, 93, 107
*Way of Being, A* (Rogers), 125
Wells, H. G., 92
Western Behavioral Sciences Institute, 126
Wolff, Antonia (Toni), 75–76,
  83n
Woolf, Virginia, 145
Wundt, Wilhelm, 25–26, 27–34
  biography of, 31–32
  and first psychology labora-
    tory, 11, 31, 33
  vs. James, 27, 28–29, 40, 44
  method of studying mental pro-
    cesses, 27, 33
  personality of, 29, 33–34
  teaching style of, 28, 32–33